Songs of the people

To Harold Gladstone Hollingworth

Brian Hollingworth   EDITOR

Songs of the people

Lancashire dialect poetry of the industrial revolution

MANCHESTER UNIVERSITY PRESS

© MANCHESTER UNIVERSITY PRESS   1977

Published by   Manchester University Press   Oxford Road, Manchester M13 9PL
ISBN 0 7190 0612 0

British Library cataloguing in publication data

Songs of the people
  1. English poetry—19th century
  I. Hollingworth, Brian
  821'.8'08   PR1221

  ISBN 0-7190-0612-0

Printed in Great Britain
by Elliott Bros. & Yeoman Ltd., Speke, Liverpool L24 9JL

Contents

The Songs of the People are voices of power.

JOHN CRITCHLEY PRINCE

Our dialectal songs and stories present themselves in the old form, full of reminiscences of the olden time. The old expressions get ready access to the feelings, and find a permanent place in the heart and memory, with the cherished ones already there existing. We do not know whether, as some one has said, "It is better to write the songs of the people than make the laws," but we are strong believers in the power of songs for good and evil. And we have little doubt that that singer has greatest influence, and is most loved by the people, who, avoiding all elaborate forms of expression and high flights of sentiment, comes to them in their own simple way, and, with their own homely phrases, weaves his songs, as it were, with a musical thread into portions of their every day life.

JOSEPH RAMSBOTTOM

Preface

I hope that this anthology of poetry in the Lancashire dialect will appeal to individual readers interested in the neglected but fascinating subject of local literature, and in particular to those interested in the little-explored but impressive phenomenon of industrial poetry in the nineteenth century. I hope also that it will be attractive to adult classes, and classes in secondary schools who are making a study of literature or social history during the industrial revolution.

There have, of course, been several previous anthologies of poems in the Lancashire dialect, though most of them have had a rather limited circulation. Among the best have been *Ballads and Songs of Lancashire*, ed. J. Harland, 1865; *Lancashire Lyrics*, ed. J. Harland, 1866; *English Lyrics and Lancashire Songs*, ed. G. Hull, 1922; *A Lancashire Anthology*, ed. May Yates, 1923; *A Lancashire Garland*, ed. G. H. Whittaker, 1936; and *A Lancashire Miscellany of Dialect Verse*, ed. J. Bennett, 1960. Many of the poems here will be found in one or more of these books.

Nevertheless where this anthology is rather different, I believe, is in its attempt to point out some of the main lines of development in dialect verse, particularly during the nineteenth century, and in its attempt to devise some new critical standards in the selection of material. Most anthologies have grouped their poems under authors, and very often treated them in strict alphabetical rather than chronological order. This seems to me to have had three disadvantages. Firstly, poets of small literary merit have been given almost as much space as the really outstanding writers in the dialect, such as Waugh and Laycock. Conversely a powerful poet such as Ramsbottom, whose best poems are rather long, has never been adequately represented. Secondly, no anthology that I have come across gives any impression of how the poets influenced one another—of how the traditional poem "Jone o' Grinfilt" was the first of a long line of similar poems, for instance, or of how major was the influence of Waugh upon later writers.

Thirdly, there is no feeling in these anthologies for the social conditions in which these poems were written: no real consideration, for instance, of the great flowering of dialect poetry which occurred during the few short years of the cotton famine in the American Civil War of the early 1860s.

I hope that by grouping the poems under thematic headings and dealing with them under these headings more or less chronologically I may have avoided some of these weaknesses. I hope, too, that the notes on the poems and the authors at the back of the anthology will help to make clear what my critical standards have been in making this selection from a huge mass of literature.

Acknowledgements

I would like to acknowledge the advice and encouragement of Brian Maidment, of Manchester Polytechnic, and Dr Peter Wright, of Salford University, in the preparation of this book, as also that of H. G Hollingworth, whose knowledge of the South Lancashire dialect was invaluable. For assistance with, and permission to reproduce, photographs I am indebted to Burnley Public Library, Manchester Public Libraries, Chethams Library, Rochdale Public Libraries, the Victoria and Albert Museum, and Frank Mullineux.

A note on reading dialect poetry

If the poems are read aloud I think that understanding dialect poetry may turn out rather more simple than reading them silently might suggest. Certainly if they are read aloud I would think that people in Lancashire, and indeed over large areas of the north of England, will have very little difficulty in understanding the general sense of a poem. The idioms, the tone of speech and the pronunciation still remain in the language, though many of the dialect words may have died.

It is important to remember that there is no standard spelling in dialect poetry. The spelling in a dialect poem is simply an attempt by the writer to imitate phonetically the sounds of his local dialect. Three things result from this. Firstly, there may be quite wide variations in spelling for what is basically the same word according to which part of Lancashire the poet comes from. A writer from north-east Lancashire like William Billington is likely to spell very differently from Edwin Waugh in Rochdale. Secondly, even poets in the same area may differ quite markedly in their spelling, according to their ear for the local accent. And thirdly, even the individual writer cannot be relied on to be consistent—a study of Samuel Laycock's poems will soon prove this.

The cheering point to be remembered in all this is that a word which may appear most outlandish when written on the printed page (as is particularly the case with Joseph Ramsbottom's poetry, for instance) will turn out to be perfectly well known and understandable when read aloud.

I hope this will help to explain what may appear to be an inconsistency in the glosses, where I have tried to give modern equivalents for certain dialectal words and phrases. In general I have done this only when it seems to me that the context of the poem does not give the reader a good chance of understanding the meaning for himself. Thus, for instance, with the dialectal pronoun "hoo" for she: in many cases it is quite obvious from the context that the poet is talking about a woman. In these cases no note is offered. Sometimes, however, the context is not clear, and then the note is given.

ILKLEY COLLEGE
LITERARY & SCIENTIFIC
ASSOCIATION.

EDWIN WAUGH, ESQ.

(THE LANCASHIRE POET),

WILL GIVE TWO HUMOROUS

READINGS

FROM HIS OWN WORKS,
IN THE COLLEGE HALL,
ON
Tuesday & Thursday Evenings,
OCTOBER 5th & 7th, 1875.

PROGRAMME, FIRST EVENING:

Part 1.

1	COMIC SONG ...	...	...	...	...	...	...	...	...
2	READING	...	...	...	...	...	"Besom Ben and his Donkey."		
3	READING	...	...	...	...	...	...	...	"Our Folk."
4	COMIC SONG ...	...	...	...	...	...	...	...	...
5	READING	...	...	...	...	...	...	...	"The Church Clock."
6	READING	...	...	...	...	...	"The Dule's i' this bonnet o' mine."		

INTERVAL OF TEN MINUTES.

Part 2.

7	COMIC SONG ...	...	...	...	...	...	...	...	...
8	READING	...	...	...	...	...	"The Old Woman's Mug."		
9	READING	...	...	...	...	...	...	"A striking Story."	
10	COMIC SONG ...	...	...	...	...	...	...	...	...
11	READING	...	...	...	...	"Come whoam to thi childer and me."			
12	READING	...	...	...	...	...	...	...	Anonymous.

ADMISSION : Reserved Seats, 1s., entrance at the College Porch ; Second Seats, 6d., at the West door.

DOORS OPEN AT 7-30, TO COMMENCE AT 8-0.

C. DENTON, STEAM PRINTER, "FREE PRESS" OFFICE, ILKLEY.

Introduction

What is poetry about? In the nineteenth century we woulld expect the subject of poetry to be the countryside, romantic places, strange and romantic characters. We would expect the subject to be the poet himself. It is surprising, therefore, to find a whole body of poetry whose main concern is the ordinary man—town dwellers in their poverty-stricken homes, unemployed workers looking for jobs, the amusements of the poor.

Yet this is exactly the subject matter of Lancashire dialect poetry, a poetry which helps to record in human terms that time of rapid economic and social change which is now called the industrial revolution. The adjective which the Lancashire writers used to described their poetry and its subject matter was always "homely". "Homely" poetry deliberately avoided the conventional and grander subjects of poetry to record the life of "simple" and unregarded men.

This is why poets like Laycock and Waugh wrote in the dialect. And this is why, even if the language they used is now fading towards obscurity, it is valuable to look again at what they wrote. They were attempting a poetry for the people in the language of the people: they attempted to capture their experiences, their thoughts and their feelings in the very language the people themselves would naturally have used.

Over the years dialect verse—like the dialect itself—has been scorned and ignored. At best it has been regarded as a quaint curiosity, a poor and unrespectable relative of true poetry. The dialect writers themselves, accepting too easily the prejudices of their betters, were often apologetic about it, and wrote in standard English when they wanted to be impressive. But now should be the time for a more serious examination of their work. Today there is a growing interest in the lives not of the rich and powerful but of ordinary, forgotten men and women. Today we are less restricted in our theories concerning the nature of literature. We no longer believe that standard English is intrinsically superior. For all these reasons, and because schools and colleges are paying more attention to studies in local social history, dialect poetry deserves to be treated more respectfully. Its value deserves to be reassessed.

This is the object of *Songs of the People*, an anthology which, I hope, will be only the beginning of further studies in dialect literature. And, since reassessment is its object, it might be worth while to begin by posing one of the most intriguing questions that has emerged from the process of collecting together the poems in this book.

Why did dialect poetry flourish so freely in industrial Lancashire in the second half of the nineteenth century? Why, particularly, was there such an outbreak of dialect writing in the few short years between 1856 and 1870? The amount of poetry produced, and its quality, in those fifteen years in the middle of the century, considering what came before and what came afterwards, are truly amazing. Three major poets, Waugh, Laycock and Ramsbottom, all wrote their best work during this period, and John Harland was able to produce his two important anthologies, *Ballads and Songs of Lancashire* (1865) and *Lancashire Lyrics* (1866). Research into dialect writing was also very keen, not only through John Harland but also with such men as W. E. A. Axon, who published his *Folk Song and Folk Speech of Lancashire* in 1870. Even in terms of literary criticism there has been little to better Ramsbottom's essay on *Writing in the Dialect*, which he wrote in 1866. Afterwards the volume of dialect writing was to continue for many years. well into the twentieth century, but its quality and its enthusiasm quickly diminished.

Why, then, should there be such a ferment of activity and creation at such a time and in such a place? One possible answer is that there was already a tradition of writing in the Lancashire dialect which went back over a hundred years, and which was not necessarily available in other areas of England. Nineteenth-century writers frequently acknowledge their debts to "Tim Bobbin," or John Collier, the eighteenth-century schoolmaster in Milnrow, who had compiled a *Glossary of Lancashire Words and Phrases* and written quite extensively in the dialect. In Lancashire, indeed, he had acted as the local Dr Johnson, and in his more limited sphere had done a great deal to make dialect study respectable. His celebrated dialogue *Tummus and Meary*, written in 1750, gained an almost classic status, and 140 years later was even advocated by an inspector for study in Lancashire schools (*cf.* note on John Trafford Clegg, p. 152).

However, it does not do to put too much emphasis on the influence of Tim Bobbin, for we must remember that the phenomenon we are describing in the 1850s and '60s was an outburst of dialect *poetry*. Now Collier himself wrote mainly in prose when he used the dialect; when writing poetry he did the respectable thing and used standard English. Moreover, whatever his influence, there is a fallow period of some seventy years between his death and the real flowering of this poetry.

Another, stronger, answer might be looked for in the influence which Robert Burns's success in Scotland had upon local writers in Lancashire. Waugh particularly was often referred to as the Lancashire Burns, and clearly he relished the title. In his commonplace book he has carefully preserved a letter from Spencer J. Hall of Burnley written in 1874. "You and your confreres [have] done for Lancashire what Burns and Hogg [have] done for the Lowlands of Scotland—you [have] immortalised a dialect and made it classical." But, again, Burns cannot provide a very satisfactory reason for what happened in the '50s and '60s. Like Tim Bobbin, Burns had been dead for over half a century when Waugh burst upon the scene, and, though Waugh was plainly influenced by Burns, much of his poetry comes from a very different tradition. Plainly the poem which made him famous, "Come whoam to thi childer an' me," has more to do with Lancashire than with Scotland.

The most satisfactory explanation, then, for the golden age I have been describing lies, I believe, not in the influence of a Collier or a Burns but in the rapid and transient movement of dialect poetry at this time from an oral tradition in which it was already well established, though poorly recorded, into a written form where it became more permanent but quickly lost its vitality.

Since it was only rarely written down, it is easy to overlook the fact that in the early years of the nineteenth century there already existed a good deal of dialect poetry. This was poetry which depended for its continuance on being passed on by song or by word of mouth. At best it might be recorded by means of penny broadsheets sold in the streets.

In 1839 John Harland wrote two fascinating articles in the *Manchester Guardian* where he carefully describes this "half literary, half oral" poetry, often recited and sung in local theatres and often "exhibited in rows upon the dead walls of our large towns where a few yards of twine, and here and there a nail driven into the mortar of the wall form the bookstand and reading desk of the lover of song amongst our industrious population" (4 Dec. 1839). Much of the poetry Harland is describing was in standard English, of course, but some of it was in dialect form. The oral tradition went back certainly as far as "Warikin Fair," which was composed in the sixteenth century, and, at the time when Harland was writing, very popular examples represented in this anthology were "Jone o' Grinfilt," "Th' Owdham weyver," "Tinker's Gardens" and "Karsy Moor."

What we see in the 1850s and '60s is a more permanent written poetry emerging from this tradition. From the 1840s onwards the movement is readily perceptible. The history of *The Songs of the Wilsons* is an excellent case in point. Most of the verse of the Wilsons—father Michael and sons

Thomas and Alexander—was composed before 1840 and was never published, except perhaps in penny broadsheets. Indeed, when the first collection was made by Alexander Wilson in 1842 he complained bitterly that so much of his father's work had been lost and forgotten. But in the next thirty years there were four editions of the poems—in 1842 and 1847, edited by Alexander Wilson, and in 1865 and 1866, edited by John Harland. A very conscious attempt was made to preserve in book form songs which, for many years previously, had been popular with working people through the oral tradition.

So the dialect poets in the '40s and '50s gradually became aware of a reading as well as a listening audience. The change was not dramatic, and old habits died hard. Procter, for instance (*Memorials of Bygone Manchester*), records that John Scholes, widely respected as a man of talent during this period, still had the habit of writing only on loose slips of paper, so that much of his work, like the Wilsons', was lost for ever.

And major poets such as Waugh and Laycock gained their inspiration, and indeed achieved their reputation, within the oral tradition. Waugh had had several very ordinary poems in standard English published and anthologised from 1850 onwards, but "Come whoam," the poem which made him famous as a dialect writer, was published first in the *Manchester Examiner*, and then achieved immense popularity as a broadsheet. All of Waugh's early poetry is intended to be *sung*, and Waugh himself in his prose descriptions of Lancashire life places great emphasis on the tradition of song in Lancashire—community singing in the mills and in the villages, and singing in the streets by small groups of people to earn money in times of hardship. Within this tradition his poetry is placed, and through this tradition his poetry became popular.

Laycock's history shows the same influences. He came to fame during the Cotton Famine of the early '60s, first by publishing in broadsheet form and in the local press, and only later in book form. His earliest poems were *lyrics* of the Cotton Famine, and, according to Milner, many of these were "learnt by heart and sung by the lads and lasses in the streets" of Stalybridge (introduction to *Collected Works*, p. x).

It seems, therefore, that the great outpouring of dialect poetry in the 1850s and '60s can best be accounted for in this way. Poets like Waugh and Laycock inherited the long-established oral tradition at just the moment when increasing literacy among ordinary people was making popular *written* poetry a more feasible proposition. By the 1860s the audience for broadsheet poetry seems to have been remarkably large, and the enforced idleness of the Cotton Famine, coupled with attempts during the famine to teach adults to read, may have made it even larger. Skeat, for instance (*Biographical List: Dialects*), estimates that Billington's "Th' Surat weyver" sold 14,000 copies during this time, and Laycock (preface to *Lancashire Rhymes*) claims 40,000 copies for his poems. Though these must be very rough calculations, they do indicate a surprisingly big readership for the decade before the first Education Act. It is in such an auspicious time, therefore, that Waugh, Laycock and Ramsbottom could flourish: "With the advent of the Wilsons, Waugh, Brierley and their contemporaries the dialect reached its palmy days. It burst into leaf and flower with astonishing quickness: 'Dow' times ripened it: newspapers boomed it" (J. Redfearn Williamson, *John Trafford Clegg*, p. 163).

However, if increasing standards of literacy encouraged dialect poetry during the "golden age" of the late '50s and '60s, they can also, I believe, be called to account for the shortness of that age and the relative decline which quickly followed. How long did the songs of the people remain the songs of the people? There is an irony in the title of this anthology which is deliberate, and which is intended to encourage the asking of just this question. My own impression is that the time was not very long.

It is remarkable, for example, how quickly the three outstanding dialect poets burnt themselves out. Waugh lived until 1890, Laycock till 1893, Ramsbottom till 1901, but almost all their effective poetry was written before 1870. Waugh remained an eminent local literary figure who even gained a Civil List pension and a place in the *Dictionary of National Biography*, but his later poetry, largely restricted to the very last years of his life, hardly retains the freshness and appeal of the poems appearing in the third edition of *Poems and Lancashire Songs* (1870). Laycock, who, unlike Waugh, wrote very little in prose, continued to write poetry throughout the '70s and '80s, but much of it is little better than doggerel. Ramsbottom seems to have written very little in any form after 1870.

This is a symptom, I think, of how quickly dialect poetry as represented in this anthology moved away from a living expression of the "songs of the people" to an antiquarian and rather nostalgic attempt to conserve a dying culture and language. For a few short years, in the '50s and '60s, the language and subject matter of the poems and the language and culture of a newly literate audience seem to have been in harmony. The new written poetry adequately represented the thoughts and feelings of the people as the poetry of the oral tradition had done. But, increasingly, higher standards of education threatened this harmony.

After 1870, as elementary education spread, the dialect and culture, at times so movingly portrayed in the poems of the preceding two decades, came more and more under attack. The correspondence which followed Inspector Wylie's suggestion that dialect should be taught in school (*cf.* p. 2, and note on John Trafford Clegg, p. 152) reveals how strongly elementary education was seen as a crusade *against* the dialect and its vivifying culture. And this had a serious effect upon both the dialect poet and his working-class audience. The poet himself was pushed on to the defensive, and his stance became increasingly that of a protector of a dying cause. Ultimately he became the purveyor of something which was

5

quaint rather than living, even to his less educated readers. His audience, on the other hand, was systematically taught to despise and root out the very language which informed such poetry, until it could hardly be regarded as respectable at all.

So, sadly and inevitably, dialect poetry in Lancashire declined. It would be unfair to suggest that there have been no worthwhile dialect poets since the days of Waugh and Laycock. Trafford Clegg in the 1890s, Sam Fitton in the early years of this century, H. B. Whitehead in the recent past and Harvey Kershaw today are all good writers in the dialect. Nor would it be right to underestimate the influence of such groups of enthusiasts as the Lancashire Authors' Association or the Edwin Waugh Society. Nevertheless we witness in the later nineteenth century, I believe, a divorce between author, subject matter and audience which was both inevitable and disastrous. The writer grows more self-conscious, begins to play with a language which he himself does not use and which a steadily diminishing number of his audience are using. The audience itself turns to the poetry not for an expression of its present feelings but for a journey into nostalgia. So the dialect form becomes less an expression of living speech and more a literary exercise. Arch references to "potato pie," "clogs" or "case clocks"—symbols of a threatened and under-esteemed way of life—begin to multiply. Moments when the feelings of ordinary people find expression in the language of the people grow less frequent.

Yet the achievements of Lancashire dialect poetry, to my mind, are real enough and should not be ignored. Dialect poetry in Lancashire has been lively, and is not yet dead. It deserves serious attention from both an historical and a literary viewpoint. It has, more than anything else, and quite unlike conventional poetry, expressed a feeling of community. The best poems of Waugh and Laycock, for instance, are marked very firmly by a delight in the oddities of people, coupled with a tolerance for their fellow men—"We're o' Johnny Butteroth's lads," says Waugh in one of his poems—which speaks for a healthy and caring community. They had inherited this feeling from the picaresque tradition of "Jone o' Grinfilt" and the Songs of the Wilsons, and this feeling is continued through such later writers as Trafford Clegg and Fitton.

Wit, too, is a mark of dialect poetry—a wit which speaks well for the human dignity of people who refused to be put down by adverse circumstances. The human situation was comical even when it was tragic. The dialect poets see clearly how people are made foolish—by pride, by love, by poverty, by old age, even by death itself—and they can laugh about it.

The best dialect poets assert the dignity of man, even when he is undignified by circumstance. They assert the quality of man, even when he is humiliated by his betters. As Laycock puts it in one of the best of his poems:

6

But deawn i'th grave, what spoils o th' sport,
No ray o'leet con shoine;
An' th' worms'll have hard wark to sort
Thy pampered clay fro' mine.

[Thee an' me]

To me the most significant difference between the dialect poetry of Lancashire and the standard English poetry of the age lies just here. In many ways dialect poetry mirrors and even magnifies the conventional weaknesses of nineteenth-century sensibility—it is often sentimental and its moral insight seems peculiarly limited. But whereas the recognised poetry of the time seems so intensely individual—the poet struggling with uncertainty, and looking for his own identity—dialect poetry speaks for the group. It is seeking, in its limited way, to find an identity, not for the poet but for "folk" thrown into a new, menacing and unprecedented social situation. The virtues it stresses are "homely" and the people it speaks to are "simple".

In this dialect poetry would be valuable if only for the voice it gives to working people, whose language has always been ignored, who are often presumed never to have spoken at all. It is valuable as a social document. But there is more to it than that. In dialect poetry at its best—in "Th' Owdham weyver," or "Bonny brid" or "Tum Rindle"—we are listening to something more than a documentary record of how it *was* to live in industrial Lancashire a century ago. Poetry speaks to the heart as well as the head, and we know how it *felt* to live there; we know what it *meant*.

It is in this belief, and in the hope that readers will be able to share something of the life of the people through their songs, that this anthology has been prepared.

7

People

Jone o' Grinfilt

TRADITIONAL

Says Jone to his woife on a whot summer's day,
"Aw'm resolvt i' Grinfilt no lunger to stay;
For aw'll goo to Owdham os fast os aw can,
So fare thee weel, Grinfilt, an' fare thee weel, Nan;
For a sodger aw'll be, an' brave Owdham aw'll see,
An' aw'll ha'e a battle wi' th' French."

"Dear Jone," said eawr Nan, un' hoo bitterly cried,
"Wilt be one o' th' foote, or theaw meons for t' ride?"
"Ods eawns! wench, aw'll ride oather ass or a mule,
Ere aw'll keawer i' Grinfilt os black os th' dule,   *hide away, devil*
Both clemmin', un' starvin', un' never a fardin', *being hungry and cold*
It'ud welly drive ony mon mad."   *almost*

"Ay, Jone, sin' we coom i' Grinfilt for t' dwell,
Wey'n had mony a bare meal, aw con vara weel tell."
"Bare meal, ecod! ay, that aw vara weel know,
There's bin two days this wick 'ot wey'n had nowt at o';
Aw'm vara near sided, afore aw'll abide it,   *decided*
Aw'll feight oather Spanish or French."

Then says my Noant Marget, "Ah! Jone, theaw'rt so whot,
Aw'd ne'er go to Owdham, boh i' England aw'd stop."
"It matters nowt, Madge, for to Owdham aw'll goo,
Aw'st ne'er clem to deeoth, boh sumbry shall know: *somebody*
Furst Frenchmon aw find, aw'll tell him meh mind,
Un' if he'll naw feight, he shall run."

Then deawn th' broo aw coom, for weh livent at top, *hill*
Aw thowt aw'd raich Owdham ere ever aw stop;
Ecod! heaw they staret when aw getten to th' Mumps,
Meh owd hat i' my hont, un' meh clogs full o' stumps;
Boh aw soon towd 'um, aw're gooin' to Owdham,
Un' aw'd ha'e a battle wi' th' French.

Aw kept eendway thro' th' lone, un' to Owdham aw went, *straight on*
Aw ax'd a recruit if they'd made up their keawnt?
"Nowe, Nowe, honest lad" (for he tawked like a king),
"Goo wi' meh thro' th' street, un' thee aw will bring
Wheere, if theaw'rt willin', theaw may ha'e a shillin'."
Ecod! aw thowt this wur rare news.

He browt meh to th' pleck, where they measurn their height, *place*
Un' if they bin height, there's nowt said abeawt weight;
Aw ratched meh un' stretch'd meh, un' never did flinch:
Says th' mon, "Aw believe theaw'rt meh lad to an inch."

Aw thowt, this'll do; aw'st ha'e guineas enoo'.
Ecod! Owdham, brave Owdham for me.

So fare thee weel, Grinfilt, a soger aw'm made:
Aw getten new shoon, un' a rare cockade;
Aw'll feight for Owd Englond os hard os aw con,
Oather French, Dutch, or Spanish, to me it's o' one;
Aw'll mak 'em to stare, like a new-started hare,
Un' aw'll tell 'em fro' Owdham aw coom.

Th' Owdham weyver   TRADITIONAL

I'm a poor cotton weaver, as many a one knows,
I've nowt to eat i' th' house an' I've worn out my cloas   *clothes*
You'd hardly give sixpence for all I have on,
My clugs they are brossen and stockings I've none,   *bursted*
You'd think it wur hard to be sent into th' world,
To clem and do th' best 'ot you con.   *starve*

Our church parson kept telling us long,
We should have better times if we'd hold our tongues,
I've houden my tongue till I can hardly draw breath,
I think i' my heart he means to clem me to death;
I know he lives weel by backbiting the de'il,
But he never picked o'er in his life.   *threw a shuttle (i.e. wove)*

I tarried six week an' thought every day wur t'last,
I tarried and shifted till now I'm quite fast;
I lived on nettles while nettles were good,
An' Waterloo porridge were best of my food;
I'm telling you true I can find folks enew,
That are living no better than me.

Old Bill o' Dans sent bailiffs one day,
For a shop score I owed him that I could not pay,
But he wur too late, for old Bill o' Bent,
Had sent tit and cart and ta'en goods for rent,   *horse*
We had nou bur a stoo', that wur a seat for two,   *only*
And on it cowered Margit and me.

The bailiffs looked round as sly as a mouse,
When they saw aw things were ta'en out ot house,
Says one to the other, "All's gone, thou may see,"
Aw sed, "Lads, never fret, you're welcome to me;"
They made no more ado, but nipp'd up th'owd stoo',
And we both went wack upo' th' flags.   *stone floor*

I geet howd of Margit, for hoo wur strucken sick,   *she*
Hoo sed hoo ne'er had such a bang sin hoo wur wick,   *alive*
The bailiffs scoured off with owd stoo' on their backs,   *scampered*
They would not have cared had they brook our necks,
They're mad at owd Bent cos he's ta'en goods for rent,
And wur ready to flee us alive.   *flay*

I sed to our Margit as we lay upo' th' floor,
We shall never be lower in this world, I'm sure,
But if we alter I'm sure we mun mend,
For I think in my heart we are both at far end,
For meat we have none nor looms to weave on,
Egad, they're as weel lost as found.

Then I geet up my piece and I took it 'em back,   *piece of woven cloth*
I scarcely dare speak, mester looked so black,   *employer*
He said, "You wur o'erpaid last time you coom,"
I said, "If I wur 'twas for weaving bout loom;   *without*
In a mind as I'm in I'll ne'er pick o'er again,
For I've woven mysel' to th' fur end."   *far*

Then aw coom out and left him to chew that,
When aw thought again aw wur vext till aw sweat,
To think that we mun work to keep them and awth' set,
All the days o' my life and still be in their debt;
So I'll give o'er trade, an' work with a spade,
Or go and break stones upo' th' road.

Our Margit declared if hoo'd cloas to put on,
Hoo'd go up to Lundun an' see the big mon,   *i.e. the king*
An' if things didn't alter when hoo had been,
Hoo swears hoo'll feight blood up to th' e'en
Hoo's nought again th' King, but likes a fair thing,
An' hoo says hoo can tell when hoo's hurt.

Th' Mon at Mester Grundy's   TRADITIONAL

Good law, how things are alter'd now,
I'm grown as fine as fippence;   *fivepence*
But when I'd used to follow th' plough
I ne'er could master threepence!
But now, why, who's so spruce as I,
When going to church o' Sundays?
I'm not poor Will o' th' yate, by Guy   *gate*
But th' mon at Mester Grundy's.

I'd us'd to stride about i' clogs,
As thick as sides o' bacon;
But now my clogs as well as hogs,
I've totally forsaken;
And little Peg I lik'd so well,
And walk'd so with o' Sundays,
I've left, and now 'tis cook maid Nell
And th' mon at Mester Grundy's.

One day I met my cousin Ralph,
Says he, "Heaw art ta, Willy?"
"Begone" (says I) "tha clumsy elf,
And dunna be so silly!"
"Why does t' forget since constant we
To market trudg'd o' Mondays?"
Says I, "Good lad, don't talk to me,
I'm th' mon at Mester Grundy's."

"Gadzooks!" (says Ralph) "Whot art ta now?
I thowt no harm i' speaking,
I've seen th' day thou wert at plough
And glad my hand t' be shaking:
But now, ecod, thou struts about
So very fine on Sundays—"
"Why, aye" (says I), "you clod, get out
I'm th' mon at Mester Grundy's."

On nice thick porridge and roast beef
At whoam I lived i' clover;   *home*
And wished such feasting while I lived,
No, never might be over;
But zounds! Did yo' but see me now,
Sat down to dine on Sundays,
Ecod, you'd stare like ony thing
At th' mon at Mester Grundy's.

Now I'm advanced fro' th' tail o' th' plough,
Like many a peer o' th' nation,
I find 'tis easy knowing how
T' forget one's former station:
Who knows, but what I may strut a squire
Wi' powdered wig o' Sundays,
Though now content to be no higher
Than th' mon at Mester Grundy's.

Friends are few when folks are poor

TRADITIONAL

When I had wark, and brass to spend
I never wanted for a friend;
Folks coome a camping every neet,   *to see me*
And moved at me when we met i' th' street.
My company wor courted then
By business folks and gentlemen;
I counted comrades by the score,
But now I've none sin' I geet poor.

I'd invitations ev'ry day
To dine or sup or tak' mi' tay,
And go and have a friendly chat
Wi' Mister this and Mistress that;
An' Squire Consequence, to boot,
Would ax me o'er to fish an' shoot
Wi' dog and gun o'er dell un moor,
But friends are few when folks are poor.

Them Scotchmen bothert me wi goods,
Wi' tongues as smooth as soft soap suds
For patronage; an' strove to get it
Wi' yards o' cloth and lots o' credit.
Bow now they've changed their tune by the mass—
They coome hawking tay for t' ready brass;
They can't see t' number on my door,—
They've gotten sae blind sin' I geet poor.

But what maes t' matter look moar faw,   *makes, look worse*
My kinsfolk doesna know me naw,—
Stuck up wi pride to sich a pitch,
They've no relations but what's rich.
For even my own brother, Jim,
Says now I'm nowt akin to him;
By gum, thinks I, naw that's a floorer,—
A mon's a boggart when he's poor.   *evil spirit*

I know there's public charity
As will not let a body dee
If he's a spirit that can strup
Ta fotchin doaf, or suppin soup;   *dough*
But I've not a nat'ral knack o' humblin',
Nor thankin' visitors for grumblin',
An' sayin' "ye please" to t' greatest bore;
They'll keep you alive, but not much moar.

So t' world wags on fro' day to day,
An' still it says, or seems to say,—
This poverty's a deadly sin,
It banishes both friends an' kin;
It stinks in every noble's nose;
An' those that's neither meat nor clooas
Mun live on th' air, an' sleep o' th' floor,
Ay, an' serves 'em reet, because they're poor.

Eawr folk

EDWIN WAUGH

Er Johnny gi's his minds to books;
Er Abram studies plants,—
He caps the dule for moss an' ferns,
An' grooin' polyants;   *polyanthuses*
For aught abeawt mechanickin',
Er Ned's the very lad;
My uncle Jamie roots i' th' stars,   *searches*
Enough to drive him mad.

Er Alick keeps a badger's shop,   *grocer's*
An' teyches Sunday schoo';
Er Joseph's welly blynt, poor lad;   *almost blind*
Er Timothy's—a foo;—
He's tried three different maks o' trades,
An' olez miss'd his tip;   *throw*
But, then, he's th' prattiest whistler
That ever cock'd a lip!

Er Matty helps my mother, an'
Hoo sews, an' tents er Joe;   *looks after*
At doin' sums, an' sich as that,
My feyther licks them o;
Er Charley,—well,—there connot be
Another pate like his,—
It's o crom-full o' ancientry,
An' Roman haw-pennies!

Er Tummy's ta'en to preitchin'—
He's a topper at it, too;
But then,—what's th' use,—er Bill comes in,
An' swears it winnut do;
When t' ones's bin strivin' o' he con
To awter wicked men,
Then t' other may's some marlocks, an'   *mischief*

Convarts 'em o'er again.

Er Abel's th' yung'st;—an'—next to Joe,—
My mother likes him t' best:
Hoo gi's him brass aboon his share,
To keep him nicely drest;—
He's gettin' in wi' th' quality,—
An' when his clarkin's done,
He's olez oather cricketin',
Or shootin' wi' a gun.

My uncle Sam's a fiddler; an'
Aw fain could yer him play
Fro' set o' sun till winter neet
Had melted into day;
For eh—sich glee—sich tenderness!
Through every changin' part,
It's th' heart that stirs his fiddle,—
An' his fiddle stirs his heart.

And when he touches th' tremblin' string,
It knows his thowt so weel,
It seawnds as if an angel tried
To tell what angels feel;
An', sometimes, th' wayter in his e'en,
'At fun has made to flow,
Can hardly roll away, afore
It's blent wi' drops o' woe.

Then, here's to Jone, an' Ab, an' Ned,
An' Matty,—an' er Joe,—
My feyther, an' my mother; an'
Er t' other lads an' o;
An' thee, too, owd musicianer,
Aw wish lung life to thee,—
A man that plays the fiddle weel
Should never awse to dee!

attempt

Tum Rindle

EDWIN WAUGH

Tum Rindle lope fro' the chimbley nook,
As th' winter sun wer sinkin';
I'm tired o' keawrin' here i' th' smooke,
An' wastin' time i' thinkin':
It frets my heart, an' racks my broo—

It sets my yed a-stewin':
A man that wouldn't dee a foo,   *fool*
Mun up, an' start a-doin'!

Then, Mally, reitch my Sunday shoon,
To rom my bits o' toes in;
An' hond mo th' jug, fro' top o' th' oon,—   *oven*
An' let mo dip my nose in!
An', come, an' fill it up again;
An' dunnot look so deawldy;   *miserable*
There's nought can lick a marlock, when   *frolic*
One's brains are gettin' meawldy.

Aw'll laithe a rook o' neighbour lads,—   *invite a crowd*
Frisky cowts, an' bowd uns;   *colts*
An' let 'em bring their mams an' dads;
We'n have it pranked wi' owd uns!   *decorated*
An' th' lads an' lasses they sha'n sing,
An' fuut it, leet an' limber;
An' Robin Lilter, he shall bring
His merry bit o' timber!

An' Joe shall come, an' Jone, an' Ben;
An' poor owd limpin' 'Lijah;
An' Mall, an' Sall, an' Fan, an' Nan,
An' Curly-pated 'Bijah;
An' gentle Charlie shall be theer;
An' little Dick, the ringer;
An' Moston Sam,—aw like to yer
A snowy-yedded singer!

I'll poo mi gronny eawt o' th' nook,
An' send for Dolly Maybo',
For when hoo's gradely donned, hoo'll look   *properly dressed*
As grand as th' queen o' Shayba;
An' little Nell shall doance wi' me,—
Eawr Nelly's yung an' bonny;
An' when aw've had a doance wi' thee,
Aw'll caper wi' my gronny!

Then, Mally, fill it up again;
An' dunnot look so deawldy;
There's nought can lick a marlock, when
One's brains are gettin' meawldy!
We're young an' hearty; dunnot croak,
Let's frisk it neaw, or never;
So, here's good luck to country folk,
An' country fun, for ever!

The little doffer

EDWIN WAUGH

A merry little doffer lad
Coom down to Shapper's mill,
To see if he could get a shop;   *place*
He said his name wur "Bill".

"Bill what, my lad?" th' o'erlooker said;
"Arto co'de nought beside?"
"Oh, yigh," said th' lad; "they co'n me things—
Sometimes,—at's bad to bide!"

"But what's thi faither's name, my lad?
Thou'll surely tell me that!"
Said th' lad, "Some co'n him 'Apple Dad',—
His gradely name's 'Owd Hat'."

"My uncle Joe's co'de 'Flopper Chop'!
An' sometimes 'Owd Betide'!
They co'n him thoose at th' weighvin'-shops;
An' I know nought beside."

Said th' o'erlooker, "I know owd Joe,—
He weighvs for Billy Grime;
But, what dun they co' *thee*, my lad,
When they co'n at *dinner-time*?"

Th' lad grinned an' said, "They never han
To co' me *then*,—no fear!"
Said th' o'erlooker, "How's that, my lad?"
Said th' lad, "*I'm al'ays theer!*"

"My lad, thou looks a lively cowt;   *colt*
Keen as a cross-cut saw;
Short yure, sharp teeth, a twinklin' e'e
An' a little hungry maw!

"But wheer hasto bin wortchin' at?
What's brought tho down *our* way?"
Said th' lad, "I wortched for Tommy Platt;
He's gan me th' bag, today."   *sack*

"Thou's brought thi character, I guess?"
Says th' lad, "Yo're wrang, I doubt;"
Says th' o'erlooker to th' lad, "How's this?"
Says th' lad, "*I'm better bowt!*"   *without*

Said th' o'erlooker, "I never see
Sich a whelp sin I wur born!
But, I'll try what I can make o' thee:
Come to thi wark tomorn!"

18

The weaver of Wellbrook

BEN BRIERLEY

Yo gentlemen o with yor heawnds an' yor parks,—
Yo may gamble an' sport till yo dee;
Bo a quiet heawse nook,—a good wife an' a book,
Is mooar to the likins o' me -e.
>   *Chorus*
>   Wi' mi pickers an' pins,
>   An' mi wellers to th' shins;   *footless stockings*
>   Mi linderins, shuttle, and yealdhook;—
>   Mi treddles an' sticks,
>   Mi weight ropes an' bricks;—
>   What a life!—said the wayver o' Wellbrook.

Aw care no' for titles, nor heawses, nor lond;
Owd Jone's a name fittin' for me;
An' gie mi a thatch wi' a wooden dur latch,
An' six feet o' greawnd when aw dee -e.
>   *Chorus*

Some folk liken to stuff their owd wallets wi' mayte,
Till they're as reawnt an' as brawsen as frogs;   *overfed*
Bo for me—aw'm content when aw've paid deawn mi rent,
Wi' enoof t' keep mi up i' mi clogs -ogs.
>   *Chorus*

An' ther some are too idle to use ther own feet,
An' mun keawr an' stroddle i' th' lone;   *crouch, straddle*
Bo when aw'm wheelt or carried—it'll be to get berried,
An' then Dicky-up wi' owd Jone -one.
>   *Chorus*

Yo may turn up yor noses at me an' th' owd dame,
An' thrutch us like dogs agen th' wo;   *push   wall*
Bo as lung's aw con nayger aw'll ne'er be a beggar,   *work hard*
So aw care no' a cuss for yoo -o.
>   *Chorus*

Then, Margit, turn reawnd that owd hum-a-drum wheel,
An' mi shuttle shall fly like a brid;
An' when aw no lunger can use hont or finger,
They'n say—while aw *could* do aw *did* -id.
>   *Chorus*

Bowton's Yard

At number one, i' Bowton's Yard, mi gronny keeps a skoo,
Hoo hasna' mony scholars yet, hoo's nobbut one or two;   *she's only*
They sen th' owd woman's rayther cross,—well, well, it may be so;
Aw know hoo boxed me rarely once, an' poo'd mi ears an' o.

At number two lives Widow Burns, hoo weshes clooas for folk;
The'r Billy, that's her son, gets jobs at wheelin' coke;
They sen hoo cooarts wi' Sam-o'-Neds's 'at lives at number three;
It may be so, aw conno tell, it matters nowt to me.

At number three, reet facin' th' pump, Ned Grimshaw keeps a shop;
He's Eccles-cakes, an' gingerbread, an' traycle beer an' pop;
He sells oat-cakes an' o' does Ned, he 'as boath soft an' hard,
An' everybody buys off him 'at lives i' Bowton's Yard.

At number four Jack Blunderick lives; he goes to th' mill an' wayves;
An' then, at th'weekend, when he's time, he pows a bit an' shaves;   *cuts hair*
He's badly off, is Jack, poor lad! he's rayther lawm, they sen,   *lame*
An' his childer keep him down a bit, aw think they'n nine or ten.

At number five aw live misel', wi' owd Susannah Grimes,
But dunno like so very weel, hoo turns me eawt sometimes;
An' when aw'm in ther's ne'er no leet, aw have to ceawer i' th' dark;
Aw conno pay mi lodgin' brass becose aw'm eawt o' wark.

At number six, next door to us, an' close to th' side o' th' speawt,   *downspout*
Owd Susie Collins sells smo' drink, but hoo's welly allus beawt;   *without*
An' heaw it is, ut that is so, aw'm sure aw conno' tell,
Hoo happen mak's it very sweet, an' sups it o hersel'.

At number seven ther's nob'dy lives, they laft it yesterday,
Th' bum-baylis coom an' marked the'r things, an' took 'em o away;
They took 'em in a donkey-cart—aw know nowt wheer they went—
Aw reckon they've bin ta'en an' sowd becose they owed some rent.

At number eight—they're Yawshur folk—ther's only th' mon
                                 an' th' woife,   *Yorkshire*
Aw think aw ne'er seed nicer folk nor these i' o mi loife!
Yo'll never see 'em foin' eawt, loike lots o' married folk,   *quarrelling*
They allus seem good-temper't like, an' ready wi' a joke.

At number nine th' owd cobbler lives, th' owd chap ut mends mi shoon,
He's gettin' very wake an' done, he'll ha' to leeov us soon;
He reads his Bible every day, an' sings just loike a lark,
He says he's practisin' for heaven—he's welly done his wark.

At number ten James Bowton lives, he's th' noicest heawse i' th' row;

He's allus plenty o' summat t' ate, an' lots o' brass an' o;
An' when he rides or walks abeawt he's dressed up very fine,
But he isn't hawve as near to heaven as him at number nine.

At number 'leven mi uncle lives, aw co him Uncle Tum,
He goes to concerts up an' deawn, an' plays a kettle-drum;
I' bands o' music, an' sich things, he seems to tak' a pride,
An' allus maks as big a noise as o i' th' place beside.

At number twelve, an' th' eend o' th' row, Joe Stiggins deols i' ale;
He's sixpenny, an' fourpenny, dark-colour't, an' he's pale;
But aw ne'er touch it, for aw know it's ruin't mony a bard,
Aw'm th' only chap as doesn't drink 'at lives i' Bowton's Yard!

An' neaw aw've done, aw'll say goodbye, an' leov yo' for a while;
Aw know aw haven't towd mi tale i' sich a fust-rate style;
But iv yo're pleas't aw'm satisfied, an' ax for no reward
For tellin' who mi neighbours are ut live i' Bowton's Yard.

Mi gronfeyther   SAMUEL LAYCOCK

Aw've just bin a havin' a peep at th' farm-heawse
Wheer mi gronfeyther lived at so long;
So aw'll draw eawt a bit ov a sketch o' th' owd spot,
And work it up into a song.
An' furst let me tell yo' aw'm sorry to foind
'At th' place isn't same as it wur;
For th' di'mond-shaped windows han o bin pood eawt,
An' they'n ta'en th' wooden latch off o'th dur.

They'n shifted that seeat wheer mi gronfeyther sat
Ov a neet when her'n readin' th' Owd Book.
An' aw couldn't foind th' nail wheer he hung up his hat,
Though aw bother'd an' seech'd for 't i' th' nook.
There's th' dog-kennel yonder, an' th' hencote aw see,
An' th' clooas-prop just stonds as it did;
There's a brid-cage hangs up wheer mi gronfeyther's wur,
But aw couldn't see owt ov a brid.

A rare foine owd fellow mi gronfeyther wur,
Wi' a regular big Roman nose;
An' though nearly eighty, he look'd strong an' hale,
An' his cheeks wur'n as red as a rose.
There wur nowt abeawt him 'at wur shabby or mean;
An' he wur no' beawt brains in his skull:

He wur allus streightforrud i' o' at he did—
An owd-fashun'd Yorkshur John Bull.

He'd a farm ov his own, an' a noice little pond,
Wheer we used to go fishin' for treawt;
An' aw haven't forgetten when th' hay time coom reawnd,
For us childer had mony a blow eawt.   *good meal*
An' when th' "heawsin" wur done, eh, we had some rare fun,   *putting the hay*
Wi' tipplin' an' rowlin' on th' stack;   [*away*
An' then mi owd gronfeyther'd come wi' his pipe,
An' we o used to climb on his back.

When aw wur a lad abeawt thirteen, or so,
Aw remember aw'd mony a good ride;
For mi gronfeyther'd getten a horse or two then,
An' a noice little jackass beside.   *male ass*
An' then he'd a garden at th' backside o' th' heawse
Wheer eawr Bobby an' me used to ceawer,
Eatin' goosbris, an' currans, an' ruburb, an' crabs,
Or owt there wur else 'at wur seawer.

Mi gronfeyther—bless him—reet doated o' me—
He'd tell me aw geet a foine lad;
An' mony a toime say, when aw'rn sit on his knee,
"Eh, bless thee; tha favvers thi dad!"
Then he'd tell mi aunt Betty to beigh me some spice;
An' whenever hoo happen'd to bake,
He'd tell her to reach deawn a pot o' presarves,
An' mak me a noice presarve cake.

God bless him, he's gone; an' a kinder owd mon
Never walk'd o' two legs nor he wur;
Th' last time aw wur o'er theer, an' seed him alive,
He coom back wi' me ever so fur.
Aw geet howd ov his hont when we parted that neet,   *hand*
An aw think aw shall never forget
Heaw he look'd i' mi face when he'rn goin' away:
It wur th' last time 'at ever we met.

A week or two after, th' owd fellow'd a stroke,—
He fell off his cheer on to th' floor;
They gether'd him up, an' they took him to bed,
But he never wur gradely no moor.
Good-bye, dear owd gronfeyther; nob'dy, aw know,
Could be fonder nor aw wur o' thee;
Aw shall never forget heaw tha patted mi yed,
When aw used to be ceawr'd on thi knee.

Cotton Fowd

SAM FITTON

We han some funny folk i' Cotton Fowd.
We'n big an' little folk, an' young an' owd;
We'n short an' tall uns too, an' fat an' smo;
So if yo' like I'll write abeawt 'em o.
Eawr Cotton Fowd ull bow the knee to noan,
It has a sort o' kingdom of its own;
We'n thick yeds, bawd yeds, bacon-yured an' curled.
It tak's o sorts o' folk to make a world.

Well, first of o, i' th' middle house,
Next dur to Rovin' Joe,
There lives a chap wi' tons o' sense,
He thinks he has it o.
Yo'll never find him worchin' hard,
He's swanky, yo' con see.   *call*
He's what they coen—howd on a bit—
I think that beggar's me.

I' th' corner house there lives a chap
Who's never tasted boose.
For, when he isno' mindin' mules,   *i.e. spinning mules*
He minds his P's an' Q's.
He's gettin' rayther wake i' th' yed,
An' wackery at th' knees.
He's brass enough to live retire;
He will do when he dees.

Next dur to him lives Bob o' Sups,
He's allus seekin' trouble,
He conno' see mich good i' life,
Unless he's seein' double.
Last week he supped his Sunday shoon,
It's time he geet some new uns.
He conno' keep his spirits up:
And what he has are blue uns.

I' that big heawse at top o' th' hill,
There lives a millionaire.
He's o his loaves an' muffins baked,
His mind is free fro' care.
There's some think he's an angel, an'
He looks it, yo' con bet.
He happen wears a halo, but
I havno fun it yet.

C

He wears tay-party whiskers an'
They hang deawn on his chest.
They say he's quite a gentleman,
I reckon he knows best.
He never looks at sich as me,
He's one o' th' upper class.
I dunno like his whiskers, but
I weesh I had his brass.

A poor owd widow lives next dur;
Hoo's welly seventy-eight.   *almost*
To keep hersel' alive at o,
Hoo fairly has to feight.
Hoo does a bit of charrin', then
Hoo goes round sellin' barm.   *yeast*
Of course hoo gets her pension, so
Hoo winno' tak' mich harm.

At number nine, next dur to t' church,
There lives a nice owd maid.
Hoo's very fond of gossipin',
Hoo mak's it in a trade.
Hoo's what they coen religious, an'
Hoo goes to t' Sunday schoo'.
If onybody plays her tricks,
Hoo'll curse 'em till they're blue.

Hoo's allus havin' bits o' fraps,   *arguments*
Wi' thoose at number seven.
By th' way hoo gets her dander up,
Hoo'll never go to Heaven.
Hoo towd a woman t' other day,
Hoo'd knock her off her perch,
But this owd maid's a chapeller,
While t' woman goes to t' church.

We han a little shop an' o,
It's kept bi Mester Cant;
He'll sell yo' owt yo' may require,
And things yo'll never want.
O' th' folks i' th' Fowd look up to him,
They sen he's gettin' rich.
It's not becose he's clever, it's
Wi' chargin' folks too mich.

O' keepin' friends wi' every one
He seems to have a knack.

24

When onybody goes i' th' shop
He smiles o down his back.
Yo' owt to yer him singin' hymns,
He gets 'em off his chest;
An' like a good church warden, he
Con sing "Amen" wi' th' best.

A widow woman lives next dur,
They coen her Mrs Green.
Hoo has a lot o' childer too,
I think hoo's seventeen.
If childer are a blessin', well,
Moor sweet 'ud be their cup,
If poor folks childer o were born
Wi' brass to bring 'em up.

We'n funny folks i' Cotton Fowd,
Some wrong, an' others reet,
They're nobbut humans after o,
There's noan of us so breet.
There's clever Dick an' crazy Joe,
An' others I could tell.
But what's the use o' sayin' moor,
Yo'n o met sich yo'rsel'!

Fairs and festivities

Warikin Fair

TRADITIONAL

Now, aw me gud gentles, an yau won tarry,
Ile tel how Gilbert Scott soudn's mare Berry.   *sold*
He soudn's mare Berry at Warikin fair;
When heel be pade, he knows not, ere or nere.

Soon as hee coom whoom, an toud his wife Grace,
Hon up wi th' kippo, an swat him ore th' face;   *long stick*
Hoo pickdt him o th' hilloc, wi sick a thwack,   *she pitched*
That hoo had whel ni a brokken his back.

Thou hooer, quo hee, wo't but lemme rise,   *whore*
Ile gi thee auth' leet, wench, that imme lies.   *information*
Thou udgit, quo hoo, but where dus hee dwel?   *idiot*
Belakin, quo hee, but I connan tel.

I tuck him to be sum gud greslmon's son;   *gentleman's?*
He spent too pense on mee when hee had doon.
He gin mee a lunch'n o denty snig py,   *eel*
An shaukdt mee bith' haundt most lovingly.

Then Grace, hoo prompdt hur, so neeat an so ne,   *got ready*
To War'kin hoo went, o Wensday betime.
An theer too, hoo stade ful five markit days,
Til th' mon wi th' mare were coom to Raunley Shaw's.

As Grace was restin won day in hur rowm,
Hoo spydt th' mon a ridin o th' mare down the town.
Bounce gus her hart, an hoo wer so glopen   *startled*
That out o th' window hoo'd like fort lopen.   *she was likely to jump*

Hoo staumpdt, an hoo star'dt, an down stairs hoo run,
Wi' th' hat under th' arm, an windt welly gon.   *breath almost gone*
Hur hed-gear flew off, an so did hur snowd,   *neckerchief*
Hoo staumpdt, an hoo star'dt, as an hoo'd been wood.   *mad*

To Raunley's hoo hy'd, an hoo hove up th' latch,
Afore th' mon had teed th' mare welly too th' cratch.   *wooden frame*
Me gud mon, quo hoo, frend, hee greets yau merry,
An desires yau'd send him money for Berry.

Ay, money, quo hee, that I connan spare:
Belakin, quo hoo, but then Ile ha th' mare.
Hoo poodt, an hoo thromperdt him, shaum't be seen;   *hit*
Thou hangmon, quo hoo, Ile poo out thin een: *eyes*

Ile mak thee a sompan, haud thee a groat,   *example, show you no*
Ile oth'r ha'th money, or poo out the throat;   *respect*

29

'Tween them they made such a wearisom din,
That for t' intreat them, Raunley Shaw coom in,

Coom fy, fy, naunt Grace, coom, fy, an a doon;   *have done*
What, deel, ar yau monkeen, or ar yau woon?   *angry?   mad*
Belakin, quo hee, yau lane so hard on—
I think now that th' woman has quite spoildt th' mon.

Coom, fy, fy, naunt Grace, coom, fy, an a doon;
Yaust ha' th' mare, or th' money, whether yau won.   *which ever you want*
So Grace got th' money, an whoomwardt hoo's gon,
Hoo keeps it aw, an gees Gilbert Scott non.

Droylsden Wakes song   TRADITIONAL

HE
It's Dreighlsdin wakes, un' wey're comin' to teawn,
To tell yo o' somethin' o' greet reneawn;
Un' if this owd jade ull lem'mi begin,
Aw'll show yo heaw hard un how fast aw con spin.
    Chorus
        So it's threedywheel, threedywheel, dan, don, dill, doe.

SHE
Theaw brags o' thisel, bur aw dunno think it's true,
For aw will uphowd thi, thy fawts aren't a few,
For when theaw hast done, un' spun very hard,
O' this awm well sure, thi wark is ill marr'd.
    Chorus

HE
Theaw saucy old jade, theawd'st best howd thi tung,
Or else aw'st be thumpin' thi ere it be lung,
Un' iv 'ot aw do, theaw'rt sure for to rue,
For aw con ha' monny o' one as good as you.
    Chorus

SHE
Whot is it to me whoe yo con have?
Aw shanno' be lung ere aw'm laid i' my grave;
Un' when ot aw'm deod, un' have done what aw con,
Yo may foind one ot'll spin os hard os aw've done.
    Chorus

Com, com, mi dear woife, aw'll not ha' thi rue,
Un' this aw will tell yo, un' aw'll tell yo true,
Neaw if yo'll forgie me for what aw have said,
Aw'll do my endavur to pleos yo' instead.
        Chorus

SHE
Aw'm glad for to yeor 'ot yo win me forgive,
Un' aw will do by yo os lung os aw live;
So let us unite, un' live free fro' o' sin,
Un' then we shall have nowt to think at but spin.
        Chorus

BOTH
So neaw let's conclude an here undeth eawr sung,
Aw hope it has pleost this numerous thrung;
Wey'll do eawr endavur to pleos yo next year
So it's threedywheel, threedywheel, dan, don, dill, doe.

Jone's ramble fro' Owdam to Karsy Moor races
MICHAEL WILSON

Come Dick, an' Nan, an' Davy,
An' sit yo' deawn be me awhile;
An' Sal, an' Mal, an' Lavy,
Aw'll tell yo' a tale 'll mak yo' smoile;
For aw've just come fro' Karsy Moor,
Wi' uncle Dan and mony moore,
'T wure cover't o'er wi' rich an' poor;
Aw never seed sich seets afoore.

Here "S and G" they'rn croying;
Theere's "Hit meh legs and miss meh pegs";
Here "yeads and tails" wurn floyink;
And there owd "garter" runs his rigs:
Here's lottery for cakes and fruit,
And theere teetotum twirls abeawt,
Wi' mony things ot's miss't; me-theawt,
Sich gams owd Nick ne'er yet fun eawt.

"Bowl up for barril't soyder,"   *cider*
Loike thunder leawd, they next did croy;
Just then, noant Nan, aw spoy'd her
Hoo'r sellink nuts—"Come, toss or buy."

31

'Aw'r gooink t' ash wot hoo did theere,
When uncle Dan bawl't i' meh ear,
"Let's goo un' have a quairt o' beer,
And suster Nan shall have her sheere."

We strudden't o'er the gorses,
An' went to th' sign o' th' "Mon i' th' Moon,"
An' theere a list o' th' horses,
An' one o' th' spoortink ladies coome;
An' whoile awr' readink which ud win,
Aw spoy'd owd Punch, wi' his lung chin,
An' his woife, Joan, wur drubbink him,
"Ecod," said aw, "we'll o goo in."

Neaw the stonds begun o-fillink,
"Walk up, walk up," the owners croy'd,
They ash'd me for a shillink,
Boh aw took me o'er to th' great hill soide.
An' neaw the horses made a start,
Oych mon o tit-back play'd his part;
It pleast meh to meh vary heart,—
Eawr Doll ne'er went so fast i' th' cart.

Neaw th' horses had done runnink,
An' nowt boh shows wurn laft to see;
Aw'd seen Punch at th' beginnink,
An' that wurn quoite enuff for me;
So aw bowt plumcakes, fill'd wi' plums,
Mich bigger far nor my two thumbs,
Hot cakes, fruit tarts, and Chelsea buns,
Meh pockets they wurn fill'd wi' crumbs.

Noant Nan hoo fell to sellink;
An' uncle Dan to drinkink went;
An' aw begun o' smellink
'Ot they wur noather want nor scant.   *lacking in money or food*
For beef an' mutton thick aw spoy'd,
An' veul an' ham on every soide,
Me guts croy'd "cubbert";—"Zouks," aw croy'd,
"Aw'll sit meh deawn an' stuff meh hoide."

Neaw fouk begun o' shiftink,
Aw fun mi in a weary cale,   *poor way*
Aw scarce could stir for riftink,   *belching*
Aw'r grown so fat wi' cakes an' ale;
Boh eh! hew thrunk! one scarce could pass;   *crowded*
Some drunk, some sober, moast beawt brass;

An' some wi' two black een by th' mass;
Whoile others ley asleep i' th' grass.

Ot last th' owd gronnam's reachink,   *grandmother's*
Hoo glendur't at meh through a ring   *stared*
An' stearted up a-preachink,—
"Eh, Jone! theaw'rt an ungodly thing."
Boh when meh story aw did tell,
Her meawth stood woide as eawr six-bell;
"By th' maskins, Jone, theaw'st pleos't meh well,
Ecod, aw'll goo next yeaar meh-sel."

Johnny Green's description
of Tinker's Gardens   ALEXANDER WILSON

Heigh! Hall o' Nabs, an' Sam, an' Sue,
Why, Jonathan, art tew theer too?
We're aw aloike, there's nowght to do,
So bring us a quart before us.
Aw'r at Tinker's gardens yusternoon,
An' whot aw seed aw'll tell yo soon,
In a bran new sung, boh it's to th' owd tune,
Yo'st ha't if yo'll join mea chorus.

Aw geet some brass fro' uncle Nat,
Eawr David lant me his best hat,
Then off for th' teawn aw seet full swat,   *sweat*
Mich faster nor Pickfort's waggins;
Aw paid meh brass, an' in aw goes,
An' eh! whot shady beawers i' rows,
Where lots o' ladies an' their beaux
Wurn set to get their baggins.   *food*

There's bonfeoirs fix'd o' the top o' pows,   *poles*
To leet yor poipes an' warm yor nose;
Then a thing to tell which way th' wind blows,
An' th' fish pond too did pleas mea:
Boh th' reawnd-heawse is the rummest shop,
It's fixt on here an' ther a prop,
Just loike a great umbrella top,
If it's not, Jimmy Johnson squeeze mea.

Aw seed a cage as big, aw'll swear,
As a wild beast show i' Sawfort fair,
There's rappits, brids, an' somethings theer,
Aw could na' gawm, by the mass, mon: *recognise*
Aw thowt o' pullink one chap's wigs,
For tellink me they're guinea pigs,
Says aw, "Mea lad, aw'm up to your rigs,   *tricks*
They're noan worth hawve o' th' brass, mon."

Aw met wi' a wench, aw'd often seen,
When aw wi' mea wark to th' teawn had bin,
Hoo're drest as foine as ony queen,
So aw just stept up behind hur:
Says aw, "Yung miss, dun yo wark fur Kay's?
Aw wove their crankys scoores o'days;"   *awkward cloth*
Hoo would no' speak, boh walk'd hur ways,
An' hoo're nowt boh a bobbin woinder.

Boh th' band o' music caps owd Nick;
Aw ne'er seed th' loike sin' aw wur wick;   *born*
Ther'n drest loike soldiers, thrunk and thick,   *massed together*
As merry as hey-makers.
Up in a tree, foive yard fro' th' greawnd,
On a greyt big table, rail'd aw reawnd,
While lads an' wenches jigg'd to th' seawnd,
"Oh, merrily danced the Quakers."

Then next aw seed a swing, by gad;
Where th' ladies flock'd loike hey-go-mad,
They wanted a roide far wor' than th' lads,
They really did, for sure.
Ther'n one wur drest so noice i' blue,
An' loike an angel up hoo flew,
Hoo'd nice red cheeks, an' garters too,
So aw thowt aw'd buck up to hur.   *approach boldly*

Aw made hur link wi' mich ado,   *link arms*
An' mounted up a great heigh brow,
Where folk run up, an' deawn it too,
Just loike March hares for sure.
So when eawr kale coom we begun,   *turn*
An' stearted off, 'twur glorious fun!
Mich faster than Cock Robin run,
When he won at Karsy Moor.

Whot wark we made aw'm shawm't to tell,
We tried, boh could no' stop eawrsel,

Till into a beawer yead-first we fell,
Where aw th' foine folk wur set, mon:
Some porter run aw deawn my shirt,
A biscuit stuck to th' lady's skirt,
An' whot wi' th' hurt, an' grease, an' dirt,
By gum, aw feel it yet, mon.

Of aw the things that pleast us, John,
Wur Tinker's heawse wi' pot dolls on:
There's Blucher an' Lord Wellington,
An' Blue Beard look'd so glum, surs;
There's Cupids under trees and shrubs,
An' men wi' harps, an' some wi' clubs,
An' naked childer up o' tubs,
Don'd eawt i' lots o' plums, surs.   *dressed*

Reet hungry, aw seet mea deawn at last,
An' swallow'd ale an' cakes so fast,
Aw wonder mea waistcoat did no' brast,
Aw'r full os mea hoide could crom, surs.   *hold*
When aw wur seen ot could be seen,   *all . . . that*
They play'd "God save eawr noble Queen";
Aw strid to th' tune reawnd th' bowling green,
An' away aw coom streight whoam, surs.

It bangs boath play-heawse, fair an' wakes,   *beats*
For gam of o' maks, ale, an' cakes,   *games of all kinds*
Aw'll bet a quart, an' theaw'st howd th' stakes,
It bangs the king's creawnation.
Aw'd ha' yo t' goo next Monday noon,
For if 't rain poikles, late or soon,   *rains heavily*
Aw'll goo again, if aw goo beawt shoon   *shoes*
For it's th' grandest place i' th' nation.

Jack, goo peawn thi fiddle   TRADITIONAL

Jack, goo peawn thi fiddle, and boy thi woife a geawn.
"Naw, aw'st ne'er peawn my fiddle for ne'er a woife i' th' teawn;
If aw wur to peawn my fiddle, aw'm sure aw should go mad,
To think what merry carrants th' owd fiddle an' me has had."   *dances*

Going to the fair

EDWIN WAUGH

Eh, Nan, Lord bless an' save us o;
Whatever's up today?
Arto boun a-dancin' in a show,
Or arto th' Queen o' May?
Thou looks a bonny pictur, wench—
I don't know how thou feels,—
Wi' thi ribbins an' thi top-knots,
An' thi fithers down to th'heels!

Eh, Sarah, mon, I'm welly done!   *almost worn out*
Six week an' never out
Fro break o' day till set o' sun;
It's knocked me up, I doubt!
Fro wark to bed, fro bed to wark;
I've had aboon mi share;
But I've broken out at last, thou sees;
An' now I'm off to th' fair.

Thou never says! Well, I declare!
It brings back to mi mind
What happened th' last time I wur theer;
An' I feel hauve inclined,—
If I can find a cheer that's fit,
An' if thou'll shut that dur,
An' come an' keawer tho down a bit,—
To tell tho how it wur.

Thous recollects our weddin'-day?
Eh, dear, I wur a swell!
I'm sure thou's not forgotten that,
For thou wur theer thisel'.
Eh, what a day we had that day!
How they did dance and sing!
An' I kept howdin' out my hond,
To let folk see mi ring.

Well, we'd just bin a fortnit wed,
When Jamie comes to me—
I could see he'd some'at in his yed
Bi th' twinkle of his e'e,—
An' he chuckt me under th' chin an' said,
Come, lay thi knittin' down;
Yon's Knott Mill Fair agate like mad,   *begun*
Let's have a look at th' town!

36

Eh, Jem, I said, thou knows reet weel
I've lots o' things to do;
But if thou wants to go to th' town;
I guess I'm like to goo.
So I dropt mi wark, an' off we went,
Donned up i' Sunday trim:
Our Jem seemed tickle't up wi' th' change,—
An' I're as fain as him. *glad*

An' when we coom to th' fairin'ground,
An' geet i' th' thick o' th' throng,
For stalls, an' shows, an' haliday folk,
We could hardly thrutch along; *push*
An' th' drums an' shouts an' merry din,—
Thou never yerd the like!
An' there nob'dy laughed much moore than me,
It fairly made me skrike! *shriek*

But a dirty pouse coom up to Jem, *slut*
An' whispert in his ear;
An' he said, "I've made my market, lass,
Thou'm talk to th' mistress here!"
That nettle't me aboon a bit;
An', as hoo're hutchin' nar, *she was moving nearer*
I grope my fist, an' said, "He's mine, *clenched*
An' touch him if thou dar!"

Our Jem wur trouble't when he seed
I took it so amiss;
So he said, "Here, Sally, let's go whoam;
We'n had enough o' this!"
An' fro' that day, now ten year gone,
We'n poo'd through thick an' thin;
But that wur th' last o' Knott Mill Fair;
For I've never bin there sin'.

Rachda Wakes   JOHN TRAFFORD CLEGG

Come, Betty, lass, it's Rachda Wakes;
Let's ramble into th' teawn,
An' feed o' brandy-snaps an' cakes,
Wi pop to wesh 'em deawn.

There's bobby-horses, dhry lond sails,
Pikin folk up i' crops,
Quack docthors wi o maks o' tales,
An' likeness-takkin' shops.   *photograph shops*

There's shootin-galleries so long
'At nobry th' end con see;
Blowing machines for wynt-pipes sthrong,
An swing-boats flyin hee.

There's cowd ice-crem, thin lemonade,
Black puddins boilt an' fried,
Wot peighs, ham sangwidges, cake brade,   *hot pies*
An' lots o' things beside.

But that's o nowt to th' penny shows—
We'll goo to them o reaund;
An' there's a circus too, tha knows,
On th' cattle-market greaund.

Th' fat woman's comn again, an' th' pig,
Th' wild-beast show, wi' th' owd smell;
An' Buckskin Billy playing tig
Wi Indians o on th' yell.   *all whooping*

Aw'll buy thee sich a fairin', lass,
As tha's ne'er had afore;
An' tha'll be th' prattiest theere, bi th' mass,
Though there'll be mony a score.

An' when it's o'er aw'll link thee wom   *take you home*
Through quiet fielt an'lone,
An' afore another Wakes con come
Wi cwortin we'll ha' done.

Th' Infirmary day
July 1890   JOHN TRAFFORD CLEGG

Come, lively lads an' laughin maids, an' folk groon up an' set,
Thrail up to th' Foxholes in a rook, an' make th'
                    brass-takkers sweat;   *a crowd*
They'n show yo lots o' gam, an' fill yor ears wi music's seaund,
An' send yo friskin like unbroken cowts o'er th' new-mown ground.

Yo'll see some bare-legged bagpipe-squeezers donned i' Heeland check,
An' one bowd fellah drop fro th' cleauds as iv he'd breighk his neck;
Yo'll see owd Punch bang folk abeaut, an' yer dog Toby yap,
Whol th' boggart comes an' lurries off th' croot ruffian deawn   *drags*
                                       th' wot gap.   *hell*

There'll be some women upo wheels, an' chaps on th' flying bar,
Some wire-walkers, an' pow-climbers, an' tuthri 'at con spar;   *pole climbers*
An' there'd ha bin some horse-sodiers, but they'n o had to bowt
An' play at babby-heause, to plez yon folk i' Lunnon fowt.   *fort*

Rowl up, an' bring o th' brass yo han, an teem it into th' box;
Its noane for th' benefit o' folk i' brodecloth an' silk frocks;
Clog-wearers han a chance this time, an'—what's not olez th' case—
Poor folk are made moore welcome nor weel-donned un's i' yon place.

We known some weel what dangers hang abeaut i' forge an' mill,   *very well*
Wheere twirlin shaft an' limber strap are swift to lame an' kill;   *quick moving*
We known some weel heaw wake an' helpless t'strongest chap con fo,
But whol we're breet an' lusty that ne'er bothers us at o.

It's when we're laid wi crippl't limbs, or brokken ribs or yeads,
Through days an' weeks o' sleepless punishment i' restless beds;
When th' engine thumps o'erweighted, an' t' valve's droppin
                                       deaan on t' breath,
An' t' doctor's kept on th' dur-step busy leggin deawn
                                       owd Dyeath;   *tripping up*

When th' wage is stopped an' th' pestil scraped,   *shank of ham*
                 an' th' breadflake bare to th' bant,   *oatcake rack bare*
When loaf and wayter han to sarve for th' wine an' beef we want;
When th' pale-faced wife creeps mournful pinin thinner day bi day,
An' clemmin childher cry for meight, too wake to laugh or play;   *starving*

When th' sick-club brass is gettin done, an' o th' stuff
                          gwone to th' pop,   *pawnshop*
Whol th' rent keeps runnin hard to catch th' long score at th' grocer's shop;
That's time to make a fellah think, an' wish he had some wit,
An gien a lift to th' hospital whol he were strong an' fit.

Th' owd days o' miracles are past, but mich con yet be done;
We cannot mend folk wi a touch, like some long dyead an' gwone,
Nor cure 'em wi a loving word—that bit o' th' knack seems lost—
But we con o be saviours yet at very little cost.

It's quare what selfish things we are at th' best, for when we're reet,
An' friskin i' th' noon sun, we never thinken o' th' dark neet;
Whol hearty we care nowt iv other folk are laid i' th' shell,
But yer us sheaut iv *they* wain't help when we're knocked deawn eaursel!

39

D.

Come then, o tender-hearted lads, an' lasses wi breet een;
Come, new-wed folk an' owd un's an' bringt' childher on to th' green;
Let's have a good owd-English day—there's noane so mony neaw—
An' for awhile stop wark an' care fro rivin us i' teaw.

Let's laugh an' sing, an' carry on as iv we'rn fairly wick,   *really lively*
Not sleauch as iv we'rn made o' stuff mixed noather thin nor thick;
An' wipe a thankful tear to know, when th' merrymakin's gwone,
We'n helped to leeten th' world a bit for some poor helpless mon.

Eawr market neet   SAM FITTON

To yo' who read as weel as run,
Eawr little town's a treat,
An' if yo' want to see some fun
Come reawnd a' th' market neet,
For if yo'll view eawr Market Square,
An' walk abeawt, a while,
Yo'll see some things to mak' yo' stare,
An' some to mak' yo' smile.

They'll sell yo' owt, eawr Market folks—
They're cute, as I con tell—
An' if yo' dunno' watch the blokes
Yo'll soon get sowd yo'rsel'.
They sell blackleads 'at winno' write,
Herb-beer 'at winno' pop;
There's apples too, yo' conno' bite,
Wi' th' ripe 'uns o' on t' top.

There's hair pins, an' there's monkey-nuts;
They'll sell yo' owt for brass,
An'—if there were no ifs an' buts—
Yo'd find it o' first-class.
There's pokers, pots, an' brandy-snaps;
There's combs to scrat yo'r nob;
There's fourpence-hawpenny warty caps   *workday*
For which they charge a bob.

There's pens an' carrots, soap an' gum;
There's pinafores an' spuds;
In short, it's just the place to come

40

For o' yo'r worldly goods.
There's nails an' slippers, shirts an' shoon,
Lead spoons an' feather-beds;
There's new-laid eggs 'at hum a tune,
Ox-tails an' hommer-yeds;   *hammer heads*

There's kettle-stands 'at winno' ston',
Gowd rings 'at are no' gowd;
There's Stilton cheese wi' whiskers on,
Cock chickens ten year owd;
There's champagne too 'at's nobbut sham,
There's bacon 'at con creep,
There's turnips labelled apple jam,
An' lamb 'at's turned to sheep;

There's fancy plants 'at winno' grow;
There's sugar, sawt an' sond;   *salt and sand*
There's Sunday socks, first-class an' o',
An' some 'at's second-hond;
There's history books an' fairy tales;
There's jokes yo' conno' see;
They'll sell yo' cakes as hard as nails,
An' teeth to chew 'em wi';

There's hankychers to wipe yo'r nose,
Screw keighs an' waggon wheels;
There's patent salve to rub yo'r toes,
An' lots o' rubber heels;
There's balls o' worsted, balls o' bant,   *twine*
A pinbow, or a pill;
There's lots o' things yo' often want,
An' some yo' never will.

We han' a Doctor Quack an' o';
He'll cure yo' in a flash;
He'll ease yo' o' yo'r gouty toe,
Yo'r colic, or yo'r cash;
He'll diagnose yo'r aches an' pains,
He'll mak' yo' think yo'r bad.
An' then he'll shift yo'r muddled brains,
An' those yo' never had;

He'll put yo' reet fro' top to toe,
He'll cure yo'r corns an' warts.
He'll shifts yo'r warchin yed an' o',   *aching*
Browt on wi suppin' quarts;
He's shifted boils i' barrowfuls—

It's true, for yo' con tell,
He's scores o' testimonials
He's written eawt hissel:

He's stuff for makkin' whiskers grow
Wheer whiskers never grew:
It's printed on a papper, so,
Of course, it must be true.
So come an' visit Doctor Quack—
He looks a gradely gawk— *a fine fool*
An' if he conno' cure yo'r back,
It's grand to yer him talk.

We han a fortune-teller too!
He's clever yo' con see,
He'll tell yo' o' yo'r beawn to do,
An' who yo'r wife 'ull be:
He'll warn yo' to be careful as
Yo' tak' a walk i' th' park:
He'll say yo'll meet a gypsy lass
Who's rayther tall an' dark;

He'll say yo'll ha' some childer too—
He fancies yo'll ha' three—
But if he knows yo'n kids enoo,
He'll tell yo' when they'll dee:
He has blue goggles o'er his een,
An' wears a cap an' gown;
He coes hissel: "Professor Green,
The Seer of world renown":
But then he's one o' th' best o' liars—
The beggar's killed wi' cheek—
He carries bobbins up at Squire's
For nineteen bob a week.

So do come up an' stop a bit,
An' see eawr little teawn;
I'll bet yo'r takken up wi' it, *pleased*
Unless yo'r takken deawn: *cheated*
An' bring yo'r wives an' childer too;
Eh, mon: it's quite a treat:
But lads, whatever else yo' do,
Yo' mun' come a' th' Market neet.

42

Owdham footbo'

AMMON WRIGLEY

It's run an' jump an' hop an' skip,
An' sheawt hooray, an' hip, hip, hip,
It's singin' songs an' eytin tripe,
An' suppin' pints at single swipe,
An' brass for th' wife to buy a hat,
An' th' childer brass for this an' that,
An' beauncin' gaily up an' deawn,
Yo' connut find a merrier teawn,
When Owdham's won.

Aw lost mi brass, awm crabbed an' croat,   *bad-tempered*
Aw lifted th' cat eawt wi' mi boot,
Awr ne'er as mad i' o mi life,
Cleautin' th' kids an' cursin' th' wife,
Awm sure mi brains han left mi yed,
Ther's nowt to do but goh toh bed,
At six o'clock o' th' Setturdy neet,
They're o i' bed i' eawr street,
When Owdham's lost.

Love

The country wedding   THOMAS WILSON

Sam, at Jack o' Neddur's, wur tir't o' livin' single life,
An' lusty Bess at Yebbur's, he towd ther fowks he'd have to wife.
"Be quiet, Sam!" th' owd daddy cries, "it's time enoof for thee t' be wed."
Co'd Sam, "Aw conno' rest my hide i' th' neet, aw feel so queer i' bed."

That neet Sam lay oneasy, an' oft for mornin' he did wish,
Until he'd seen his Bessy he couldn't look at porridge dish;
His loom stood still, an' he look't ill, and every day he thinner grew:
At last th' owd daddy gav' consent, and joyfully to Bess he flew.

When Bess receiv'd the welcome news, a modest blush
                              proclaim'd her charms;
And Sam was smit with Cupid's dart, and round her neck he threw his arms;
He buss'd and kiss'd her o'er and o'er, while Bessy, fainting, hung her head.
At last keen nature ceased to throb, and both agreed i' th' morn to wed.

I'th' morn Sam wakken'd Bess by time, and likewise Tom an' Jer an' Joe,
An' Bill an' Dick, an' Ned an' Jack; each had a lass wi' him to go.
A fiddle too, Sam swore he'd have, and to owd blind Jud he gav' a crown;
With "Tink-a-tink," an' "Bob an' Joan" so merrily they jogg'd to town.

With pleasant chat they ownward jog, aich lad did clip his bonny lass;   clasp
An' when they coom to th' Half-way House, Sam paid for aich
                              a thumpin' glass.
With merry hearts again they start, and in town they now arrive;
To th' church they goo, by two an' two, an' boldly to the altar drive.

Now little scowlin' Joshua comes, the wedding folks throng in the aisle,
An' with his gown an' book he stands: Sam wink't an' Bess hoo gan a smile.
The knot wur tied, then home they hied, blind Jud wi' the fiddle led the van,
The neighbours welcomed their return, an' join'd 'em in the flowin' can.

Now th' lads they fell to doncin', an' lasses join'd 'em in th' fun,
Exceptin' Bess, who linger'd an' nudged at Sam, an' whisper'd, "Come."
Blind Jud struck up, "Off she goes," an' Sam cried, "On, wi' o' my heart."
No doubt Sam donced i' double time, an' Bess, aw'm sure,
                              hoo play'd her part.

The neighbours they coom flockin' in, and happiness did wish the pair.
An' to conclude the weddin' feast, blind Jud wi' th' fiddle banish'd care;
Sam paid for o' th' weddin' fees; with cake an' ale they did regale;
An' to this day, wife Bess agrees, that Sam in love does never fail.

The Lancashire witch   JOHN SCHOLES

An owd maid aw shall be, for aw'm eighteen to-morn,
An' aw'm 'yen to keep sengle an' free;   *I'm eager*
But the dule's i' the lads, for a plague they were born,
An' thi' never con let one a-be, a-be,
They never con let one a-be.

Folk seyn aw'm to' pratty to dee an owd maid,
An' 'at luv' sits an' laughs i' my ee;
By-leddy! aw'm capt' 'at folk wantin' to wed;   *astonished*
Thi' mey o tarry sengle for me, for me,
Thi' mey o tarry sengle for me.

There's Robin a' Mill,—he's so fond of his brass,—
Thinks to bargain like shoddy for me;
He may see a foo's face if he looks in his glass,
An' aw'd thank him to let me a-be, a-be,
Aw'd thank him to let me a-be.

Coom a chap t'other day o i' hallidi' trim,
An' he swoor he'd goo dreawn him for me;
"Hie thi whoam furst an' doff thi," aw sed, "bonny Jim!   *get undressed*
Or thae'll spuyl a good shute, does-ta see, does-ta see,   *suit*
Thae'll spuyl a good shute does-ta see."

Cousin Dick says aw've heawses, an' land, an' some gowd,
An' he's plann'd it so weel, dun yo' see!
When we're wed he'll ha' th' heawses new-fettled an' sowd,   *repaired*
But aw think he may let um a-be, a-be,
Sly Dicky may let um a-be.

Ned's just volunteer'd into th' "roifle recruits,"
An' a dashin' young sodiur is he;
If his gun's like his een, it'll kill wheer it shoots,
But aw'll mind as they dunnot shoot me, shoot me,
Aw'll mind as they dunnot shoot me.

He sidles i' th' lone, an' he frimbles at th' yate,   *fumbles at the gate*
An' he comes, as he coom no' for me;
He spers for eawr John, bo' says nought abeawt Kate,   *asks*
An' just gi'es a glent wi' his ee,
An' just gi'es a glent wi' his ee.

He's tall an' he's straight, an' his curls are like gowd,
An' there's summat so sweet in his ee,
'At aw think i' my heart, if he'd nobbut be bowd,   *bold*
He needna' quite let me a-be, a-be,
He needna' quite let me a-be.

The dule's i' this bonnet o' mine

EDWIN WAUGH

The dule's i' this bonnet o' mine;
My ribbins'll never be reet;
Here, Mally, aw'm like to be fine,
For Jamie'll be comin' to-neet;
He met me i' th' lone t'other day,—
Aw're gooin' for wayter to th' well,—
An' he begg'd that aw'd wed him i' May;—
Bi' th' mass, iv he'll let me, aw will.

When he took my two honds into his,
Good Lord, heaw they trembled between;
An' aw dursn't look up in his face,
Becose on him seein' my een;
My cheek went as red as a rose;—
There's never a mortal can tell
Heaw happy aw felt; for, thae knows,
One couldn't ha' axed him theirsel'.

But th' tale wur at th' end o' my tung,—
To let it eawt wouldn't be reet,—
For aw thought to seem forrud wur wrung;
So aw towd him aw'd tell him to-neet;
But, Mally, thae knows very weel,—
Though it isn't a thing one should own,—
If aw'd th' pikein' o' th' world to mysel',
Aw'd oather ha' Jamie or noan.

Neaw, Mally, aw've towd thae my mind;
What wouldto do iv 'twur thee?
"Aw'd tak him just while he're inclined,
An' a farrantly bargain he'd be;
very good
For Jamie's as greadly a lad
As ever stept eawt into th' sun;—
Go, jump at thy chance, an' get wed,
An' ma'e th' best o' th' job when it's done!"

Eh, dear, but it's time to be gwon,—
Aw shouldn't like Jamie to wait;—
Aw connut for shame be too soon,
An' aw wouldn't for th' world be too late;
Aw'm o ov a tremble to th' heel,—
Dost think 'at my bonnet 'll do?—
"Be off, lass,—thae looks very weel;—
He wants noan o' th' bonnet, thae foo!"

What ails thee, my son Robin?   EDWIN WAUGH

What ails thee, my son Robin?
My heart is sore for thee;
Thi cheeks are grooin' thinner,
An' th' leet has laft thi e'e;
Theaw trails abeawt so lonesome,
An' looks so pale at morn;
God bless tho, lad, aw'm soory
To see tho so forlorn.

Thi fuustep's sadly awter't,—
Aw used to know it weel,—
Neaw, arto fairy-stricken, lad;
Or, arto gradely ill?
Or, hasto bin wi' th' witches
I' th' cloof, at deep o' th' neet?
Come, tell mo, Robin, tell mo,—
For summat is not reet!

"Eh, mother, dunnot fret yo;
Aw am not like mysel';
But, 'tisn't lung o' th' feeorin'   *because of the things to be frightened of*
That han to do wi' th' deil;   *devil*
There's nought 'at thus could daunt mo,
I' th' cloof, by neet nor day;—
It's yon blue een o' Mary's;—
Thay taen my life away."

"Aw deawt aw've done wi comfort
To th' day that aw mun dee,
For th' place hoo sets her fuut on,
It's fairy greawnd to me;
But, oh, it's no use speykin',
Aw connut ston her pride;
An' when a true heart's breykin'
It's very hard to bide!"

Neaw, God be wi' tho, Robin;
Just let her have her way;
Hoo'll never meet thy marrow,   *equal*
For mony a summer day;
Aw're just same wi' thi feyther,
When first he spoke to me:
So, go, thi ways, an' whistle;
An' th' lass 'll come to thee!

49

Come, Mary, link thi arm i' mine

EDWIN WAUGH

Come, Mary, link thi arm i' mine,
An' lilt away wi' me;
An' dry that little drop o' brine,
Fro' th' corner o' thi' e'e;
Th' mornin' dew i' th' heather-bell's
A bonny bit o' weet;
That tear a different story tells,—
It pains my heart to see't.
    So, Mary, link thi arm i' mine.

No lordly ho' o' th' country side's   *hall*
So pleasant to my view,
As th' little corner where abides
My bonny lass an' true;
But there's a nook beside yon spring,—
An' if theaw'll share't wi' me;
Aw'll buy tho th' bonny'st gowden ring
That ever theaw did see!
    So, Mary, link thi arm i' mine.

My feyther's gan mo forty peawnd,
I' silver an i' gowd;
An' a pratty bit o' garden greawnd,
O' th' mornin' side o' th' fowd;
An' a honsome bible, clen an' new,
To read for days to come;—
There's leaves for writin' names in, too,
Like th' owd un at's awhoam.   *at home*
    So, Mary, link thi arm i' mine.

Eawr Jenny's bin a-buyin' in,
An' every day hoo brings
Knives an' forks, an' pots; an' irons
For smoothin' caps an' things;
My gronny's sent a kist o' drawers,   *chest*
Sunday clooas to keep;
An' little Fanny's bought a glass
Where thee an' me can peep.
    So, Mary, link thi arm i' mine.

Eawr Tum has sent a bacon-flitch;
Eawr Jem a load o' coals;
Eawr Charlie's bought some pickters, an'
He's hanged 'em upo' th' woles;

Owd Posy's white-weshed th' cottage through;
Eawr Matty's made it sweet;
An Jack's gan me his Jarman flute,   *German*
To play bi th' fire at neet!
        So, Mary, link thi arm i' mine.

There's cups an' saucers; porritch-pons,
An' tables greyt an' smo';
There's brushes, mugs, an' ladin'-cans;
An eight-day's clock an' o;
There's a cheer for thee, an' one for me,
An' one i' every nook;
Thi mother's has a cushion on't,—
It's th' nicest cheer i' th' rook.   *of all*
        So, Mary, link thi arm i' mine.

My gronny's gan me th' four-post bed,
Wi' curtains to't an' o';
An' pillows, sheets an' bowsters, too,
As white as driven snow;
It isn't stuffed wi' fither-deawn;
But th' flocks are clen an' new;
Hoo says there's honest folk i' th' teawn
That's made a warse un do.
        So, Mary, link thi arm i' mine.

Aw peeped into my cot last neet;
It made me hutchin' fain;   *restlessly happy*
A bonny fire were winkin' breet
I' every window-pane;
Aw marlocked upo' th' white hearth stone,   *danced up and down*
An' drummed o' th' kettle lid;
An' sung, "My neest is snug an' sweet;
Aw'll go and fotch my brid!"
        So, Mary, link thi arm i' mine.

Coaxin'   JOSEPH RAMSBOTTOM

Hi thi, Jenny, lyev thi loom,
There's a bonny sky above;
Eawt o' th' days we wortch to live,   *work*
We may tak a day to love.
Wilto stop thi bangin' lathe;

Come away fro th' neighsy jar;
Let thi shuttle quiet lie,
For thi bobbins winno mar.   *won't get spoiled*

Fling thi clogs an brat aside;   *apron*
Let thi treddles rest to-day;
Tee thi napkin o'er thi yead;
Don thi shoon an' come away.
Everlastin' tugg un teighl,
If eawr lives mun so be spent,
What's the good o' whistlin' brids?
Why wur posies ever sent?

Deawn bi th' well, at th' hollow oak,
Under th' hawthorn blossom sweet,
Wheer a linnet sings above,
An' a rindle runs at th' feet;   *stream*
An' the red rimm'd daisies look
Wi' their gowden een int' heaven,
An' eawr gronnies used to tell
Ut the little fairies liven,

Theer we'll sit, an' talk o' th' time
Ut we so mich wish ud come,
When we'st find it reet to wed;
When we'st have a tidy whoam,
Wi' sich lots o' babby smocks,
An sich rows o' clogs an' shoon,
An' sich breeches, skirts, an' frocks;
Why—it conno come too soon.

If aw ha t' goo eawt t' mi wark,
Thea'll noa miss me for a day,
When thea's hauve-a-dozen tongues
Prattlin' reawnd while aw'm away;
An' a dozen pattherin' feet
Racin' into th' loane ull come;
They'll be fain to meet their dad
When they known he's comin' whoam.

O, the skips, the jumps, the romps,
An' the little songs they'll sing;
Thea'll be th' graceful queen o' th' hearts,
Lass, an' aw'st be th' jolly king.
So neaw come an' lyev thi loom,
Ther's a bonny sky above;
Eawt o' th' days we wortch to live,
We may tak' one day to love.

Stop wi' thi mother JOSEPH RAMSBOTTOM

Yo'n throuble wi' childher fro' th' cayther to th' grave, *cradle*
Yo fend for, an' nuss 'em, an' teighl like a slave,
Bo soon as they thinken they win their own bread,
Yer's some crazy maggot gets into their yed,
They're fondlin' an' foo'in'
An' billin' an' cooin',
An' never con sattle bo gwon an' get wed.

A that'ns eawr Harry's for doin', aw see;
He's sowt him a sweetheart, an' cares no' for me,
Young Tamar o' Tatty's neaw has him i' play,
Hoo's won him, an' wean'd him, an' lyeds him away,
For o' aw'm his mother,
He tells me t' noa bother,
An' nobbut keeps laughin' at owt 'at aw say.

Hoo lives wi' her gronny i' th' Ellison Broo;
They pike up a livin' bi owt they con do,
Bi keepin' a mangle an' bakin' wutcakes, *oatcakes*
An' doctherin' childher for faintins an' shakes.
Th' owd woman's great larnin'
I' yarbs, an' hoo's arnin' *herbs,*
A torin' on livin' bi th' sauves 'at hoo makes. *a poor living, medicines*

He roots into books, an' he bothers wi' schoos,
An' talks abeawt Moses an' Aaron an' thoose,
An' fumbles wi' figures, an' moithers his yed *bothers*
Wi' o' maks o' things 'at'll bring him no bread.
Aw've nowt agen schooin',
Bo folk should be doin'
'At han t'arn a livin' an' myen to get wed.

Whate'er win they do, for he gets no mich brass?
Yer's nowt bo hard wark an' hard clemmin' for th' lass,
An' huddlin' i' rooks i' their livin' like hogs. *crowds*
Hoo mun powler abeawt in ther bedgeawn an' clogs, *must go rambling*
Till want ull bewildher
Bwoth them an' their childher,
An' powfagg'd an' famish'd they'n o' gwo to th' dogs. *worn out*

Bo Harry, my lad, if thea'd yer som'dy tell
What thrials an' throubles thea'll bring o' thisel,
If nobbut for once thea'd ha sense to be said,
An' rid o' this rubbish, lad, eawt o' thi yed,
Yer's sich lots o' warnin'
Thea'd surely tak larnin',
An' stop wi' thi mother, an' never get wed.

53

Neaw aw'm a married mon   JOSEPH BURGESS

When mi faythur fust wur wed,
A cheer, un a stoo',
A table, un a bed,
Wur reckont things enno;
Bu' neaw it costs so mich
A heawse o' goods to get
That if you arno' rich
Yo're forc't to run i' debt.

Yo' happen think it low
This marryin' short o' brass,
Un mi yed desarves a jow   *knock*
For bein' sich an ass:
Bu' seven i' every eight,
I' these days ut we're amung,
If they'rn bund to marry streight,
Wudno' ha' to marry yung.

They'd ha' to scheme un scrape,
Till they'd gettun yallow skins,
Till ther shoothers lost ther shape,   *shoulders*
Un ther noses toucht ther chins;
Bu' me un my yung woife
One another loikt too mich
To waste th' best yers o' loife
I' waitin' whoile wer'n rich.

Un as hoo's a factory lass
Un me a factory lad,
We'n noather on us brass—
Aw nobbu' weesh we had;
Soa we'st booath ha' to work,
Un it wudno' be so fair
If aw began to shirk,
Un didno' do mi share.

Soo aw'st help to mop un stone,   *scour with a donkey stone*
Help to scrub un skeawr,
Un do everythin' aw'm shown,
If it lies within mi peawer;
Fur, neaw aw'm a married mon,
Aw'm beawn to be soa good,
Un do the best aw con
To be o' a husbant should.

Aw reckon aw'st ha' t' rock,   *i.e. a cradle*
Un larn t' mak cinder tay,
At three or four o' clock,
When it's happens breakin' day;
Un other odds un ends,
Sich as hurryin' eawt foot whot,   *hotfoot*
When a loife or two depends
Upo' foindin' Dr Scott.

Well, if trouble cooms wi woives,
Pleasure cooms as weel,
To leetun warty loives,   *working*
Un mak us happy feel;
Un aw've awlus yerd it sed,
Bi thoose aw think should know,
That we owtno' trouble dread,
For th' pleasure pays for o'.

Aw know there's lots to do
Before we safely float,
But we'st manage if we poo
Together in one boat;
Un aw dunno' feel a deawt
But fro' danger we'st be screen'd,
Very soon be eawt,
Un never look beheend.

Soa we'll tak things as they coom
Wi' an undaunted pluck,
Un awlus be awhoam
To every sooart o' luck;
Never wear a freawn,
Or drink fro' sorrow's cup,
Whether up i' th' wo'ld or deawn,
Whether deawn i' th' wo'ld or up.

If we hanno' th' wo'ld i' bants,   *conquered the world*
We'n faith enoof t' believe,
We'st nare ha' mony wants
That we hanno' means t' relieve;
Soa aw'll finish for this toime,
But, as shure as aw'm a mon,
Tell yo' sum day else, i' rhyme
Heaw mi woife un me gan on.

Yon weyver as warks t' beeam to me

WILLIAM BARON

I' t' shed, wheer aw'm toilin' an' slavin'
Fro' mornin' to neet, like a foo';
An' piecin' mi bad sides an' "mashes,"   *broken threads*
Till aw wonder which way aw ged throo,
There's a lass, hey! so winsome an' pratty,
An angel yo'd tek hur to be;
An' at me hoo throws lots o' sly glances,
For hoo only just warks t' beeam to me.   *on the facing loom*

Hoo comes to hur wark dressed i' t' fashion,
For hoo's fondish o' mekin' a show;
Hoo weears a silk jacket to weyve in,
An' a watch, an' a locket an' o.
Hoo struts like a princess throo th' alley,
Or some lady wi' titles an' gowd;
An' hur hair used to hang o'er hur eye broos,
But lately hoo's getten id powd.   *cut*

If ther's ever a ball hoo'll be at id,
An' bi wod aw've heeard other fooak say,
At dancin' a "polka" or t' "lancers,"
Ther's few as con lick hur today.
An' aw'm towd hoo's a bit uv a singer,
Wi' a voice 'at's so soft an' so sweet;
But if ther's a thing hoo delights in,
It's flashin' hursel' uv a neet.   *showing off*

Hoo'll nod speyk to t'other young lasses,
As warks on to t' looms reawnd abeawt;
For because they dorn'd weear lots o' finery
Hoo thinks they're below hur, no deawt.
Let hur think sooa, for may be id suits hur,
But this aw con truthfully say:
Aw'd sooner hev one plain an' hooamly,
Than fifty like hur, ony day.

Aw know 'at hoo's hed lots o' fella's,
Aw'll bet as they'd number a scooar;
For them as aw've sin hur misel' wi
'Ud mek up a dozen, or mooar.
An' id strikes me hoo thinks aw'st swell t' number,
Bi' t' way as hoo smiles o' t' day throo,
But hoo'll find as hoo's rayther misteken,
If hoo thinks 'at aw'm nowt but a foo'.

56

Aw pity thad fella as gets hur,
For he'll not hev much pleasure i' life;
Hoo's a long way to preawd, an' too giddy,
To ever mek owt uv a wife.
If hoo heeard hawf 'at fooak ses abeawt hur,
Hur cheeks 'ud blush t' colour o' t' rooase;
For they say 'at hoo corn'd darn a stockin',
Nor fasten a patch on hur clooas.

Then let hur keep smilin' an' glancin'
To wheedle me reawnd if hoo con;
If hoo's fishin' abeawt for a greenhorn,
Hoo'll hev to try some other mon.
Aw find single life growin' lonesome,
An' ther'll soon be a weddin', yo'll see,
But aw've picked eawt a far better partner,
Than yon weyver as warks t' beeam to me.

Eawr Sarah's getten a chap   SAM FITTON

Eh, dear; there's bin some change in
Eawr heause this week or two;
Wheer once there used to be a din
It's like a Sunday schoo';
We never feight for apple pie,
We very seldom frap;   *lose our temper*
An' what d'ye think's the reason why?
Eawr Sarah's getten a chap.

Eawr fender shines just like a bell,
We'n had it silvered o' er;
An' th' cat appears to wesh itsel'
Moor often than before;
Eawr little Nathan's wiped his nose,
Eawr Jimmy's brushed his cap;
An' o this fuss is just becose
Eawr Sarah's getten a chap.

He's one o' thoose young "nutty" men,
They sen he's brass an' o,   *say*
My mother's apron's allus clen,
For fear he gives a co;   *a call*
We'n polished up th' dur knocker, too;
We'r swanky yo' con tell;

57

But Sarah says it winno do,
We'st ha' to have a bell.

We bowt a carpet t'other neet,
To wear it seems a sin;
My feyther has to wipe his feet
Before he dar' come in;
He never seems a'whoam someheaw,
He says he's noan on th' map;
He allus wears a collar neaw
Eawr Sarah's getten a chap.

We'n serviettes neaw when we dine;
A brand new bib for Ben;
Eawr Fanny's started talkin' fine,
Wi' lumps in neaw an' then,
Sin' Sarah geet her fancy beau
Hoo fairly cocks her chin;
Hoo has a bottom drawer an' o
To keep her nick-nacks in.

Hoo's wantin' this, an' wantin' that,
Hoo thinks we're made o' brass;
Hoo goes to th' factory in her hat,
Hoo says ut it's moar class;
Hoo's bucked my feyther up shuzheaw,   *anyhow*
He darno' wear a cap;
He gets his 'bacco chepper neaw
Eawr Sarah's getten a chap.

He comes o' courtin' every neet,
He fills eawr cat wi' dread;
He's sky-blue gaiters on his feet,
An' hair-oil on his yed;
He likes to swank about an' strut
An' talk abeawt his "biz";
He's "summat in an office," but
I don't know what it is.

His socks are crimson lined wi' blue,
I weesh he'd do a guy;   *clear off*
I weesh he'd pop the question, too,
Or pop his yallow tie;   *pawn*
My feyther darno' raise a row,
An' th' childer darno' scrap;
We feel to live i' lodgin's neaw
Eawr Sarah's getten a chap.

58

He's put eawr household in a whirl,
He's sich a howlin' swell;
I weesh he'd find another girl,
Or goo an' loose hissel';
Eawr parrot's gone an' cocked its toes,
Eawr roosters conno' flap;
We'er gooin' daft an' o becose
Eawr Sarah's getten a chap.

Eawr Joe

H. B. WHITEHEAD

Eawr Joe he's started coortin' neaw,
Un' dons his-sel i' state;   *dresses*
Yoh'd never think he work't ut mill,
Un piec't i' th' jinny-gate;
Yoh'd hardly know him neaw-o'-days,
He's eawt o' th' common rut;
In fact he's what us workin' foak
U'd co' a gradely nut.

For when he's finish't uv a neet,
Un' gets whom froo his wark,
Yond clogs o' his ur eawt o' th' seet,
Un hud away i' th' dark;
Then when he sits deawn toh his tay,
Aw connot help but grin,
He wants a cup un' saucer neaw,
Un' his slices cuttin' thin.

He's donn'd op every neet i' th' week,—
Froo seven ut clock till eight
He stonds ut front ut th' looking glass,
To get his toppin streyt;   *hair*
He'll stroke it o'er un bruysh it back,
Until it shines like lard,
Then sprinkles it wi' scented stuff,
Ut kills at fifty yard.

Yoh'n yerd 'em swank o'er Owdham Park,
Un't fleawers ut are its;
Yond pair o' socks o' eawr Joe's
Con lick it into fits;
King Solomon 'ud never nowt

Like yond inside his shoon
He's just like a woakin' green-heawse   *walking*
On a Sundi' afternoon.

Ther's forget-mi-knots, un daisy cheeons,
Un' things aw ne'er sin groo;   *grown*
Wi' sprigs o' lad's love heeor un theeor
O' work't i' green un blue;
Un' yond he's started coortin' wi'
He co's his "wild mawss rose,"
Hoo's op un deawn wi' hair ut's bobb'd,
Un peawder on her nose.

Ho'll hardly speyk toh me ut o,
Just nods un sez, "How doo,"
Then puts her finger tips toh mine,
Un mak's mi feel a foo';
Hoo's op toh date i' o hoo does,
O' that ther's noh mistake;
But then, wi' o' her swank un style,
It's odds hoo connot bake.

Then when he brings her toh her tay,
It fairly nettles me;
Ther's lots o' things on't table neaw,
Ut didn't used toh be;
But if it doesn't awter soon,
Awm beawn toh pack mi trunks,
Awm feeor fed up, wi' sich like stuff,
The'r jellies un' the'r chunks.

Thi goh'n i' th' parlour when thi'n done,
Un don't forget toh stop;
Thi noather seem toh know nor care,
Who does th' weyshin' op;
Theeor thi sittun howdin' honds,
As sawft as thi con be,
It met bi th' road ut coorters does,
But looks queer wark toh me.

He tak's her whom agen ut neet,
Gets back ut twelve-ut-clock;
Aw bin asleep two heawrs then,
As seawnd as onny rock;
When in creeps Joe, as cowd as ice,
Un puts his feet o' me,
Then shuvs mi eawt o' my warm shop,
As hard face't as con be.

Aw never get noh gradely rest,
Wol th' dawn begins toh peep;
For when he's gettun warm i' bed,
He's toakin' in his sleep;
Ther's lots o' things ut aw could tell,
He thinks aw dunnot know;
But then it hardly would bi reet;
Remember he's eawr Joe.

Home

An old toast

TRADITIONAL

Meight when we're hungry;
Drink when we're dry;
Brass when we're short on't,
An' heaven when we die.

Come whoam to thi childer an' me

EDWIN WAUGH

Aw've just mended th' fire wi' a cob;
Owd Swaddle has brought thi new shoon;
There's some nice bacon-collops o' th' hob,
An' a quart o' ale-posset i' th' oon;   *oven*
Aw've brought thi top-cwot, doesta know,
For th' rain's comin' deawn very dree;   *drearily*
An' th' har-stone's as white as new snow;—
Come whoam to thi childer an' me.

When aw put little Sally to bed,
Hoo cried, 'cose her feyther weren't theer,
So aw kiss'd th' little thing, an' aw said
Thae'd bring her a ribbin fro' th' fair;
An' aw gav' her her doll, an' some rags,
An' a nice little white cotton-bo';
An' aw kiss'd her again; but hoo said
'At hoo wanted to kiss *thee* an' o.

An' Dick, too, aw'd sich wark wi' him,
Afore aw could get him upstairs;
Thae towd him thae'd bring him a drum,
He said, when he're sayin' his prayers;
Then he looked i' my face, an' he said,
"Has th' boggarts taen houd o' my dad?"
An' he cried whol his e'en were quite red;—
He likes thee some weel, does yon lad!

At th' lung-length, aw geet 'em laid still;
An' aw hearken't folks' feet that went by;
So aw iron't o' my clooas reet weel,
An' aw hang'd 'em o' th' maiden to dry;   *clothes horse*
When aw'd mended thi stockin's an' shirts,
Aw sit deawn to knit i' my cheer,
An' aw rayley did feel rayther hurt,—
Mon, aw'm *one-ly* when theaw artn't theer.

64

"Aw've a drum an' a trumpet for Dick;
Aw've a yard o' blue ribbin for Sal;
Aw've a book full o' babs; an' a stick,   *pictures*
An' some 'bacco an' pipes for mysel;
Aw've brought thee some coffee an' tay,—
Iv thae'll *feel* i' my pocket, thae'll *see*;
An' aw've bought tho a new cap to-day,—
For aw al'ays bring summat for *thee*!

"God bless tho' my lass; aw'll go whoam
An' aw'll kiss thee an' th' childer o' round;
Thae knows that wheerever aw roam,
Aw'm fain to get back to th' owd ground;
Aw can do wi' a crack o'er a glass;   *chat*
Aw can do wi' a bit of a spree;
But aw've no gradely comfort, my lass,
Except wi' yon childer an' thee."

Neet-fo   EDWIN WAUGH

Th' wynt blows keen through th' shiverin' thorns,
An' th' leet looks wild i' th' sky;
Come, Tet, stir up that fire; an' draw
That keyther gently by;   *cradle*
I've done my weshin', gronny; an' I've tidied everything,
An', neaw I'll sit me deawn to sew,
An' hearken th' kettle sing.

Bring in some coals; an' shut that dur,—
It's quite a wintry day;
Reitch deawn that ham: for Robin likes
A relish to his tay.
Sweep th' grate; an' set yon table eawt;
Put th' tay-pot upo' th' oon;   *oven*
It's gettin' on for baggin'-time,   *tea-time*
An' he'll be comin' soon.

The fire bruns clear; an' th' heawse begins
A-lookin' brisk an' breet,
As th' time draws near when he gets back
Fro' teawn at th' edge o' neet;
It makes one hutch wi' glee to yer   *twitch*
A favourite fuut come whoam;
An' it's very fine to hearken, when
One thinks it's sure to come.

Th' cat pricks up her ears at th' sneck,   *door latch*
Wi' mony a leetsome toot;   *look*
An' th' owd arm-cheer i' th' corner seems
As if it yerd his fuut;
Th' window blinks; an' th' clock begins
A-tickin' leawd an' fain;
An' th' tin things winkin' upo' th' wole,—   *wall*
They groon as breet again.   *twice as bright*

Th' kettle's hummin' o'er wi' fun—
Just look at th' end o' th' speawt;
It's like a little sooty lad
That's set his lips to sheawt:
Th' wayter-drops 'at fo'n fro' th' tap,
Are gettin' wick wi' glee;   *coming alive*
An' yo're fain, gronny, too,—I know,—
But noan as fain as me!

Keep th' rockers gooin' soft and slow,
An' shade that leet away;
I think this little duck's o' th' mend,   *getting better*
Hoo sleeps so weel to-day;
Doze on, my darlin'; keep 'em shut,—
Those teeny windows blue;
Good Lord; if aught should happen thee,
What could thi mammy do!

Here, gronny, put this cover on,
An' tuck it nicely in;
Keep th' keyther stirrin' gently; an'
Make very little din:
An' lap those dimpled honds away   *fold*
Fro' th' frosty winter air;
They lie'n a-top o' th' bit o' quilt,
Like two clock-hommers theer!   *clock-hammers*

But stop; hoo's laughin'! Come, hie up,—
My bonny little puss!
God bless it! Daddy's noan far off;
Let mammy have a buss!   *kiss*
He's here! Tet bring that cheer!
Eh, dear; these darlin's two!
If it wur not for this chylt an' him
What could a body do!

Margit's comin'

EDWIN WAUGH

Eh! Sam, whatever doesto meeon?
Aw see thaw'rt theer i'th nook again,—
Where aw've a gill thae's nine or ten;
Hast dropt into a fortin?   *fortune*
Aw wonder heaw a mon can sit
An' waste his bit o' wage an' wit:
Iv aw're thi wife, aw'd make tho flit,—   *move*
Wi' little time to start in.

But, houd; yo're Margit's up i' th' teawn;
Aw yerd her ax for thee at th' Crown;
An' just meet neaw, aw scamper't deawn—   *and just now*
It's true as aught i'th Bible!
Thae knows yo're Margit weel, ov owd;
Her tung,— it makes mo fair go cowd
Sin' th' day hoo broke my nose i' th' fowd   *village*
Wi' th' edge o' th' porritch thible.   *porridge stirrer*

It's ten to one hoo'll co' in here,
An' poo tho eawt o' th' corner cheer;
So, sit fur back, where th' runnin's clear;—   *where you can get away*
Aw'll keep my e'en o' th' window;
Thae'm mind thi hits, an' when aw sheawt,   *you must watch your chance*
Be limber-legged, an' lammas eawt;   *run away*
An', though hoo'll not believe, aw deawt,
Aw'll swear aw never sin tho.   *saw*

Aw'll bite my tung, aw will, bi th' mon;   *by the man (i.e. Jesus)*
Aw'll plug my ears up, till hoo's gone;
A grooin' tree could hardly ston
A savage woman flytin';   *scolding*
If folk were nobbut o' i' th' mind   *could only agree*
To make their bits o' booses kind,   *resting places (i.e. homes)*
There'd be less wanderin' eawt to find
A corner to be quiet in.

It's nearly three o'clock bi th' chime:
This ale o' Jem's is very prime;
Aw'll keawer mo deawn till baggin'-time,   *tea time*
An' have a reech o' bacco;
Aw guess thae's yerd o' Clinker lad
An' Liltin' Jenny gettin' wed;
An' Collop gooin' wrang i' th' yed,—
But, that's nought mich to crack o'.   *talk about*

67

There's news that chaps 'at wore a creawn,
Are getting powler't up an' deawn;   *knocked about*
They're puncin' 'em fro' teawn to teawn,
Like foot-bo's in a pastur';
Yon Garibaldi's gan 'em silk;   *beaten them finely*
Th' owd lad; he's fairly made 'em swilk;   *swish about*
An' neaw, they sen he's sellin' milk
To raise new clooas for Ayster.   *Easter*

There's some are creepin' eawt o' th' slutch,
An' some are gettin' deawn i' th' doitch;   *ditch*
Bi th' mon, aw never yerd of sich
A world for change o' fortin'!
They're gooin' groanin' eawt o' th' seet,
They're comin' cryin' into th' leet;
But, howd! aw yerd, o' Monday neet,
A tale abeawt a cwortin'.

Poo up! aw'll tell it iv aw con;
Thae knows that little bow-legged mon,
But heigh,—owd lad! yo'r Margit's yon,—
Hoo's comin' like a racer!—
Some foo has put her upo' th' track;
Cut, Sam; hoo'll have us in a crack!
Aw said hoo'd come,—let's run eawt th' back;
Bi th' mass, aw dar not face her!

Dinner time   EDWIN WAUGH

The wife comes running into the house

Heigh, Mary; run for the fryin'-pon;
An reitch that bit o' steak;
I see thi faither comin', yon;
Be sharp; for goodness sake!
He's as hungry as a hunter;
An' there'll be a bonny din
If he finds o' out o' flunter   *everything at sixes and sevens*
An' nought cooked, when he comes in!

"Lord, bless my life; why, th' fire's gone out!
Whatever mun I do?
Here, bring a match, an' a greasy clout,   *rag*
An' a bit o' chip or two: *firewood*
An' look for th' ballis: doesto yer?   *bellows*

68

They're upo' th' couch, I think;
Or else they're hanged a-back o' th' dur;
Or else they're under th' sink.

"An' tak' those dish-clouts off that cheer;
An' shift yon dirty shoon;
An' th' breakfast things are stonnin' theer;
Put 'em a-top o' th' oon;
Be sharp; an' sweep this floor a bit:
I connot turn my back,
To speighk to folk, but o' goes wrang,
An' th' house runs quite to wrack

"These chips are damp: oh, Lord o' me!
I'm sure they'n never brun:
There's no poor soul's warse luck than me
That's livin' under th' sun!
Now then; what keeps tho stonnin' theer;
Hangin' thy dirty thumbs?
Do stir thy shanks; an' wipe that cheer;
It's no use; here he comes!"

The husband comes in from work

"By th' mass; this is a bonny hole,
As ony i' this town!
No fire; no signs o' nought to height;   *eat*
Nowheer to sit one down!
I have to run whoam for a meal,
When th' bell rings at noontide,
An' I find th' house like a dog-kennel:
Owd lass, it's bad to bide!

"Thou's nought to do, fro' morn to neet,
But keep things clean an' straight,
An' see that th' bits o' cloas are reet,
An' cook one's bit o' meight;   *meat*
But thou's never done it yet, owd lass:
How is it? Conto tell?
Thou mends noan, noather; an', by th' mass,   *you don't get any better either*
I doubt thou never will!

"It's quite enough to have to slave
Fro' soon i' th' day to dark;
An' nip, an' scrat, an' try to save,   *take small meals*
An' no thanks for one's wark:
No wonder that hard-wortchin' folk

Should feel inclined to roam
For comfort to an alehouse nook,
When they han noan at whoam.

"I'm fast: I don't know what to say;
An' I don't know what to do;
An' when I'm tired, at th' end o' th' day,
I don't know where to goo.
It makes me weary o' my life
To live i' sich a den:
Here, gi's a bit o' cheese an' loaf,
An' I'll be off again!"

Down again!   EDWIN WAUGH

'Twur on a bitter winter neet,
When th' north wind whistled cowd;
When stars i' th' frosty sky shone breet,
An' o' wur still i' th' fowd;
I'd getten curl't up snug i' bed,
An' sleepin' like a top,
When Betty nudged my ribs, an' said,
"Oh, Jamie; do get up!"

I yawned, an' rubbed my e'en, an' said,
"Well, lass, what's th' matter now?"
Then Betty rocked hersel' i' bed,
An' said, "Get up, lad; do!"
"It's woint that troubles tho," said I,   *wind*
"Thou'd better have a pill."
"Oh, Jem," said hoo; "don't be a foo;
Thou knows what makes me ill!"

"Howd on, my lass," said I; "howd on!"
An', bouncin' out o' bed,
I began to poo my stockin's on:
"Oh, do be sharp!" hoo said;
But, my things had gone astray i' th' dark;
An', as I groped about,
Hoo said, "Oh, this is weary wark;
Thou'll ha' to goo without!"

"Goo wheer? Wheer mun I goo?" said I,
As I rooted upo' th' floor: *searched about*
"Goo wheer?" said hoo; "thou leather-yed;

70

For th' doctor, to be sure!"
"Eh, aye," said I: "thou'rt reet, by th' mass!
An' if thou'll make a shift   *effort*
To tak thi time a bit, owd lass,
Thou's have him in a snift!"   *jiffy*

I donned my things, an' off I went
Like shot, through th' frosty neet;
Wi' nought astir but th' wintry woint,   *wind*
An' nought but stars for leet:
An' as through th' dark an' silent fowd,
My clatterin' gate I took,
I spied owd Clem, crept out o' th' cowd,
With his lantron, in a nook.

"What's o' thi hurry, Jem?" said he,
As I went runnin' by:
"I connot stop to talk to thee;
We'n someb'dy ill," said I.
"Who is it this time?" cried owd Clem;
"Is it Nan, or little Ben?"
"Nawe, nawe," said I, "it's noan o' them;
Our Betty's down again!"

"Well done," cried Clem," well done, owd lad!
Why that makes hauve a score!"
"It does," said I; "that's what we'n had;
An' we's happen ha' some moore."
"Never thee mind, my lad," cried Clem;
"It's a rare good breed, owd mon;
An' if yo han a hundred moore,
God bless 'em every one!"

Th' doctor wur up in hauve a snift;
An' off I scutter't back,
Like a red-shank, through the wintry drift,   *bare-legged person*
Wi' th' owd lad i' my track.
Th' snow wur deep, an' th' woint wur cowd
An' I nobbut made one stop,
At th' little cot at th' end o' th' fowd,
To knock her mother up.

I never closed my e'en that neet,
Till after break o' day;
For they kept me runnin' o' my feet,
Wi' gruel, an' wi' tay:
Like a scopperil up an' down i' th' hole,   *spinning top*

I're busy at th' owd job,
Warmin' flannels, an' mendin' th' fires
An' tentin' stuff o' th' hob.   *looking after*

It wur getten six or theerabout;
I're thrang wi' th' gruel-pon;   *busy*
When I dropt mi spoon, an' shouted out,
"How are yo gettin' on?"
"We're doin' weel," th'owd woman said;
"Thou'd better come an' see;
There's a fine young chap lies here i' bed;
An' he wants to look at thee!"

I ran up i' my stockin'-feet;
An' theer they lay! By th' mon;
I thought i' my heart a prattier seet
I ne'er clapt e'en upon!
I kissed our Betty; an' I said,—
Wi' th' wayter i' my e'en,—
"God bless yo both, my bonny lass,
For evermoore, Amen!

"But do tak care; if aught went wrang
I think my heart would break;
An' if there's aught i' th' world thou'd like,
Thou's nought to do but speak:
But, oh, my lass, don't lie too long;
I'm lonesome by mysel';
I'm no use without thee, thou knows;
Be sharp, an' do get weel!"

Eawr Jack   J. W. MELLOR

Ther's tay kettle singin' a tune,
An' th' babby's i' th' krather asleep;
Eawr Jack'll bi comin' whoam soon,
Aw'll look sharp an' get o' made reet,
He'd sanner see owt upside deawn   *sooner*
Nor th' place wheer he sits ov a neet.

Thoose candlesticks shinin' up theer,
Aw rubbed at 'em rarely today;
For when he sits deawn in his cheer,
He's sure to look up fro' his tay,
Wi'—"What hasto gotten up theer?

72

Laycook

Welcome Bonny

Bud

They dazzle like sunleet i' May!"

An' th' floor, too, aw've dotted it o'er
Wi' snow-spots, they met ha' just fone;   *fallen*
Aw'm sure it's so weel covert o'er,
Ther's nobody 'ud think it wur stone,
An' though aw've oft said it afore,
Ther's no clanner cottage i' th' lone!

He worches reet hard for us o',
Aw'm one 'at con see an' con feel;
But yet aw should like him to know,
His wife worches hard too as weel,
An' iv wi'n bin deawn rayther low,
Wi'n kept a fuut awlus o' th' wheel.

Theer! neaw o's made reet, he may come!
He'll throw his e'en smilin' o' th' floor;
He's preawd ov his lass an' his whoam,
He's said so, an' who could say mooer?
"Neaw, mother!"—Well?—"Fayther's i' th' lone!"
Then let's go an' meet him at th' dooer.

Weh lad! thae looks jaded toneet;
Eh, dear! thae's bin slavin' away
"Aw think so has theaw; look heaw breet!—"
Come! come! sit thee deawn to thy tay!
"No fear but awst awlus bi reet
While theaw smiles as sweet as today!"

Welcome, bonny brid   SAMUEL LAYCOCK

Tha'rt welcome, little bonny brid,
But shouldn't ha' come just when tha did;
 Toimes are bad.
We're short o' pobbies for eawr Joe,   *bread soaked in milk*
But that, of course, tha didn't know,
 Did ta, lad?

Aw've often yeard mi feyther tell,
'At when aw coom i' th' world misel'
 Trade wur slack;
And neaw it's hard wark pooin' throo—
But aw munno fear thee,—iv aw do   *mustn't frighten*
 Tha'll go back

Cheer up! these toimes 'll awter soon;
Aw'm beawn to beigh another spoon—   *going to buy*
        One for thee;—
An', as tha's sich a pratty face
Aw'll let thi have eawr Charley's place
        On mi knee.

God bless thi, love! aw'm fain tha'rt come,
Just try and mak' thisel' awhoam:
        Here's thi nest;
Tha'rt loike thi mother to a tee,
But tha's thi feyther's nose, aw see,
        Well, aw'm blest!

Come, come, tha needn't look so shy,
Aw am no' blamin' thee, not I;
        Settle deawn,
An' tak' this haupney for thisel',
Ther's lots of sugar-sticks to sell
        Deawn i' th' teawn.

Aw know when first aw coom to th' leet,
Aw're fond o' owt 'at tasted sweet;
        Tha'll be th' same.
But come, tha's never towd thi dad
What he's to co' thi yet, mi lad,
        What's thi name?

Hush! hush! tha mustn't cry this way,
But get this sope o' cinder tay
        While it's warm;
Mi mother used to give it me,
When aw wur sich a lad as thee,
        In her arm.

Hush-a-babby, hush-a-bee,—
Oh, what a temper! dear-a-me
        Heaw tha skrikes!   *shrieks*
Here's a bit o' sugar, sithee;
Howd thi noise, an' then aw'll gie thee
        Owt tha likes.

We've nobbut getten coarsish fare,
But, eawt o' this tha'll get thi share,
        Never fear.
Aw hope tha'll never want a meal,
But allus fill thi bally weel   *belly*
        While tha'rt here.

74

Thi feyther's noan been wed so lung,
An yet tha sees he's middlin' thrung   *rather crowded*
        Wi' yo' o.
Besides thi little brother Ted,
We've one upsteers, asleep i' bed,
        Wi' eawr Joe.

But tho' we've childer two or three,
We'll mak' a bit o' reawm for thee,
        Bless thee, lad!
Tha'rt th' prattiest brid we have i' th' nest,
So hutch up closer to mi breast;
        Aw'm thi dad.

Wimmen's wark es niver done

(As if bi a womman hersel)   JAMES STANDING

Aw dunnot reckon aw con preytch,
Aw ne'er were treyn'd to do't,
Yet may be aw cud make a speech
If aw were reyt put to't;
At least aw've lang'd sometimes to try,
An' neaw aw've like begun,
An' this es th' text aw've ta'en i' hand—
"Wimmen's wark es niver done."
O'th Monday morn aw get up tired—
A child tug, tug at th' breast;
Aw think sometimes aw'd lig whol eight,   *stay in bed till eight*
But really ther's no rest.
Bi th' workers get off to ther wark
Another lot begin
To romp abeawt, an' feight, an' heyt   *hit*
An' make a wary din;
One's sheawtin—"Mother, do get up
An' come an' lick eawr John,   *spank*
He's makin' sugar-butter-cakes,
An' leyin' treycle on;
Eawr Billy's been i' th' cobberd top   *cupboard*
An' brokken th' fancy plate
Ut yo tell'd us we mudn't touch—
Yo'd put it eawt o' th' gate."   *out of the way*
An' then eawr Betty's rooitin' up   *searching round*
I' th' box ut should be fast;   *shut*
Eawr Tommy's runn'd eawt in his shirt
An's makin' cakes wi nast.   *dirt (i.e. mud pies)*

75

This way they carry on ther pranks,
An' make ther rows i' th' heawse,
Whol aw'm plump foarc'd to get op too,   *just*
For talkin's ov no use.
Aw've then to buckle to mi wark,
For aw've so mich to do
Whol't ligs i' yeps o' ivery side,   *while it lies in heaps*
An' plenty on't for two.
Wi' th' young un skrikin' i' mi arms,
Aw do th' jobs as aw con:

Aw've th' breakfast first of all to make,
An' th' childer's clooas to don;
Then two or three mun off to th' schooil,
An' that i' time an' all;
Or else they'll say they dar'not go
An' sit ther deawn an' bawl.
Th' clock then strikes nine afoor aw've t'chonce
To get a bite o' meyt.   *food*
A mother's no chance fur hersel'
Whol th' child's eawt o' th' gate.   *until, out of the way*
It's reyk mi this, an' fotch mi th' tother,   *reach*
Gie mi that, an' bring another,
This button stitch, that gallus sew,   *pair of braces*
This shirt sleeve mend—it's all i' tew;
An' mony a scoor o' little jobs
'At aw con hardly mention,
That all tak op a mother's time,
Her patience an' attention.

Bi th' time aw get mi child asleep,
Aw've then to start an' shap   *get ready*
To make a dinner o' some kind
Whol th' babby gets a nap;
When in come two or three fro' th' schooil,
An' start o' roatin' eawt—   *bellowing*
"Han yo hetten all t' parkin up?
Aw'll bet yo'n laft me beawt."
Aw've then to grin, an' stamp, an' feight,
An' jowl ther yeds together;
An' spite ov all they wakken th' child
An' cause mi endless bother;
So that aw coan't ha' th' dinner made
Bi th' tother lot come in;   *before*
Aw've then their freawnin' looks to tak',
Beside their plaguey din.

76

Mothers Union

Wimmen's work es
niver done

Page 77

They niver seem to think it aught
Heawiver aw've to run,
An' niver seem to gie't a thought
Ut my wark's niver done.

Aw think sometimes aw should be made
To do beawt rest or bed,
Wi double hands at ether side,
An' een all round mi yed: *eyes*
Aw cudn't then mind ivery point,
An' keep all corners reyt—
Wheer ther's a rook o' childer kept
Yo' connut keep things streyt.
I'th afternoin aw'm thranged wi' wark   *overbusy*
Aw've ne'er no time to leyk;   *relax*
Ther's weyshin' deys an' cleanin' deys,
An' deys to cook and bake,
An' mony a hundred bits o' jobs
'At mothers han' to do.
Ther's weyshin' up, an' mendin' stuff,
An' th' bit o' nursin' too;
But th' creawnin' point ov all, aw think,
Is after six at neet.
A'a! what a pantomine ther is!
It'ld cap yo' all to see 't.
One sits i' th nook, its face awry
An' makin' sich a din—
It's yerd a hurdy-gurdy chap,
An' neaw it's practisin'.
Another's seen some huntin' dogs,
An's looin' like a heawnd,   *baying*
Or sheawtin' like th' owd huntin' chap—
It seems to fancy th' seawnd.
Then one or two 'at's deawn o' th' floor
Are usin' all ther brains
To puff an' blow, an' yell an' crow,
Like whistlin' railway trains.
Another batch o' th' bigger end
Are jackin' o'er ther wark,   *giving up*
Or playin' bits o' crafty tricks,
To have a merry lark.
At th' end of all they disagree,
An' then, folks, A'a, what bother!
One turns to bein' meysterful,
An' starts o'cleawtin' t'other.

Aw've then to start an' feight mysel',
For tawkin's eawt o'date;

They've getten hoofed wi't, like th' owd chap,   *used to it*
An' laugh to yer mi prate.
An' as for him, he takes no part
I' keepin' corners square;
Heawiver heedless th' childer be,
He niver seems to care;
An' stead o' leyin' on a hand,
An' helpin' what he con,
He leovs all t' bits a jobs to me,
Whol mi warks niver done.
At last ov all they get to bed,
Aw'm some an' feyn to see 't,   *very glad*
For it's a comfort to be quiet
An heawr or two at neet.
Aw wish sometimes aw had been born
Below a lucky star,
Wi' all mi looaves an' muffins baked,
Like th' gentle folks's are.
But then, agen, aw think, for sure
All persons have ther ills;
We'd just as weel be killed wi' wark,
As dee wi' takin' pills.
Then when aw look at th' childer's cheeks
It brings joy to my heart,
Aw tak' a noble pride to think
Aw act a woman's part.
An' though aw ha' no halls nor lands
'At aw mi own con call,
Aw'm blest wi' childer fresh an' fair,
An' that eawtweighs 'em all.

Th' childer's holiday   SAM FITTON

Eh, dear, I'm welly off my chump!
I scrub, an' wesh, an' darn;
Eawr childer han a holiday,
An th' heawse is like a barn.

Yo talk abeawt a home sweet home!
My peace is flown away;
I have to live i' Bedlam for
A fortnit an' a day.

They're in an' eawt from morn to neet,
I met weel look so seawer;
They're wantin' pennies every day,
An' butties every heawer.   *bread and butter*

They'n worn my Sunday carpet eawt
Wi' runnin' up an' deawn;
Eawr Polly broke a jug today,
An' Jimmy broke his creawn.

They'n nobbut bin a-whoam a week,
But, bless me, heaw they grow;
An' talk o' childish innocence,
The devil's in 'em o.

They'n smashed a brand new dolly tub,
An' o' my clooas pegs;
They'n rattled th' paint off th' parlour door,
An' th' skin off th' table legs.

They started pooin' th' picters deawn,
One neet when I were eawt,
Eawr Tum geet th' "Rock of Ages," an'
He gave eawr Joe a clout.

Eawr Bill, who has a biggish meawth—
He's allus in disgrace—
Set off cowfin' t'other day,
An' went reet black i' th' face.

He'd swallowed th' babby's dummy-tit
Wi rawngin' wi eawr Bet;   *romping*
We'n gan him tons of physic, but
We hanno fun it yet.

Eawr Jack's a plester on his nose,
An' th' beggar looks a treat;
He'd pood his tongue eawt to a lad
Who lives i' Stoney-street.

Eawr Bobby's bin i' bed o day,
Poor lad, he does look hurt.
He went o' bathin' yesterday,
An' some'dy stole his shirt.

79

They're o so full o dirt an grime,
I'st never get 'em clen;
I'st ha' to scrape 'em when it's time
To go t' schoo again.

Eawr Tommy says he winno' goo,
That lad's a wary wight.
He's had his thumb, i' th' mangle, an'
He swears he conno' write.

clever fellow

I sat me deawn o Wednesday neet,
An' th' parson's wife were theer.
I hope hoo didno yer me swear—
They'd put a pin i' th' cheear.

I'd lock 'em up i' th' schoo for good
If I could ha' my will;
I'd see they had another clause
I' th' Education Bill.

I've clouted 'em an' slapped 'em till
My honds an' arms are sore;
I'st fancy I'm i' Paradise
When th' holidays are o'er.

They're like a lot o lunatics,
They'n getten eawt of hond;
But yet, I wouldno part wi' em
For o there is i' th' lond.

Work

TO THE
MasterManufacturers
OF MANCHESTER AND ITS NEIGHBOURHOOD.

Gentlemen,

The Committee, acting in the name and on the behalf of the Quilting Weavers' Union, respectfully beg leave to request, that you will take into serious consideration the wretched condition of your Operatives, doomed as we are to incessant labour, without the necessary means of subsistance, and compelled to bear the insults and reproaches of others, who (without more labour) are better fed and better clothed than ourselves: yet still, we are not so sunk in the scale of rational beings, nor so void of sensation, but we keenly feel the double weight of insult and oppression.

It has been the invariable practice of our Masters, of late years, on the slightest indication of a slack Trade, to make that a ground for the Reduction of Wages, and the plausibility of the pretext has always had the desired effect, till, by repeated deductions, we are brought to a state bordering on absolute want.

It requires but a small exertion of intellect to perceive that, if our Masters are justified in lowering wages in a slack trade, it must be equally just, on our part to expect an advance when the trade becomes brisker; but we are sorry to say, that now the cause is wholly removed, the effect still remains, and all our endeavours to obtain an amendment to our wages, have been regarded with the coldest indifference. In this situation we have ventured to make our appeal, in hopes that a sense of justice, and of what is due to humanity, will induce you to take our case into immediate consideration. We beg leave also to state, that the practice of taking a yard or more from every piece weaving, without paying for the same, is contrary to the laws of England, and is completely at variance with every principle of fair dealing between man and man.

We have also taken the liberty to state, fairly and candidly, that an advance of seven shillings on the pound upon the annexed prices, and likewise upon all descriptions of Quilting not included in this list, cannot be deemed unreasonable; for, in the event of obtaining it, our earnings would be far below those of other Mechanics, and upon a fair computation of labour, would not average more than Fifteen Shillings per Week.

In hopes you will not allow us to remain a prey to distress and insult,

We remain, yours respectfully,

(By Order of the Committee,)

WM. HUNTINGTON, PRESIDENT.
GEO. BRADSHAW, SECRETARY.

LIST OF OUR PRESENT PRICES:

					s.	D.
80 Reed	1 Shuttle,	36 Diamonds,	per yard,		3	2
70 do.	do.	32 do.	-	do.	2	1
66 do.	- do.	26 do.	-	do.	1	4
60 do.	- do.	26 do.	-	do.	1	3
54 do.	- do.	20 do.	-	do.	0	10½
48 do.	- do.	16 do.	-	do.	0	8

Manchester; printed by M. WILSON, Barlow's Court, Market-street.

Rambles in Owdham, and peep into the workshops

TRADITIONAL

When I'd finished off my work
Last Saturday at neet,
Wi' new hat and Sunday clooas
I dress'd myself complete;
I took leeof o' my mother
Wi' a very woful face,
And started off for Owdham soon,
That famous thriving place.

When I geet to Coppy Nook,
It pleos'd me reet well,
I seed all the town ofore me,
O' which I'm goin to tell;
There wur coaches, carts, and coal-pits,
As throng as you'd desire,
And coal enough they'rn gettin' up
To set th' whole town o' fire.

I coom up to th' Owd Church,
And I seed th' New Market Hall,
It looked so queer o buildin'
I couldn't help but call;
One part of it their'n settin' out
Wi' very pratty shops,
They'n lined it wi' cast iron,
And they'n built it upo' props.

I then went down below,
And then how I did stare,
To see so mony folks
Un' so mony sorts o' ware;
I'm sure I think that Braddock
Is o vast affrontin' chap,
For t' put folk into the' cellar
When they set up keepin' shop.

To Hibbert and Platt's shop
I went i' th' Lackey Moor,
Un' fun no little trouble
To get in ot th' Lodge door;
And then by gum so busy
They wur at it left and right,
Un' stripp'd in all their shirts too,
'Ot I thought they're goin' to fight.

Some chaps 'ot they caw'd Smiths,
Great bellows they had got,
Like foos they blow'd *cow'd* wind,
To make their iron *hot*;
But then owd Neddy Engine,
I think he beats the whole;
He's fond o' *summot warm* sure   *something*
For they feed him upo' coal.

The Moulders, omong sand
Wur makin' things complete,
Fro' o shaften or o fly wheel,   *shaft*
To o handsome fire grate.
Cast iron's very dear now,
Or it would be nought wrong,
To make some scolden' woman
O new cast iron tongue.

I went to Barns's next,
Un' just looked through some rooms,
Where some wur making spring frames,
Un' others power looms.
Some turnin' un' some filin',
Un' screwin' bolts to beams;
I reckon soon both sun and moon
They'll make to go by steam.

I went to lots o' Fact'ries
To see what they'rn obout;
I couldn't get to see much there,
Because they'd all turn'd out.   *gone on strike*
They would not gi' them brass enough,
As far as I could learn;
Un' so th' turnouts wur goin' about,
O lookin' for th' short turn.

I went into a weavin' shade,   *shed (factory)*
Un' such o clatter there!
Wi' looms un' wheels all going so fast,
I hardly durst go near;   *dare*
Then the lasses wur so busy
Shiftin' temples—shuttlin' cops;
One shuttle had liked o given me   *almost gave*
O devilish slap o t'chops.

I went to other workshops,
Some of which I didn't know;

I remember Green's and Hallody's,
Garnet's and Sam Roe's;
I wanted t' see o chap ot Travis's;
But there I're much i th' fault
For they said all th' chaps wur fuddlin'   *drinking*
Down at Collitt's Vaults.

I coom again up th' town,
Reet opposite "Swan" door,
Un' there I yeard an organ,
Like a lion it did roar;
Un' folk wur all o crowdin'
Up stairs there just like a station;
I said, sure there's a church here;
They'n o famous congregation.

I wanted to see all,
So I clammer'd up o loft,
Un' to show 'ot I'd good manners,
My hat I quickly doft;
But when the singing started
I stood just like o gobbin   *clown*
For instead of "Hallelujah",
They blow'd out "Gee, wo Dobbin."

When I fun it wur o alehouse,
I sit me down i' th' throng,
When o chap 'ot they caw'd Bardsley
He sung o rare good song;
Un' when he coom to th' end on't
They gan him some fine claps;
There wur chaps for lasses lookin' out,
Un' lasses for their chaps.

If th' workfolk will be reasonable,
Un' th' *measters but be just*,
The turn outs will all *turn in*,
Un' prosper all sides must;
For your lasses they are pratty,
Your workmen rare and clever;
So success to Owdham town an' trade,
Un' th' workin' folk for ever.

The factory worker's song   TRADITIONAL

Come carders an' spinners an' wayvers as weel,
Stop yo'r frames an' yo'r jennies, strip roller an' creel;
Let yo'r lathes cease to swing, an' yo'r shuttles to fly,—
For there's gone through owd England a leaud battle-cry,—
    Derry deawn!

They'n turned eaut at Ratchda' an' Owdham an' Shay
An' th' Stalybridge lads are at Ash'n today;
"Fair wage for fair work" is the motto they'n chose,
An' what'll be th' upshot no mortal man knows.
    Derry deawn!

Eawr mesthers are screwin' eaur noses to th' dust,
An' if we don't strike we'n no' maybe seen th' wust;
They've cheeant up eaur bodies to slavery's wheel,
And they'd sell, if we'd let 'em, eaur souls to the diel.
    Derry deawn!

The factory bell   EDWIN WAUGH

Come, Billy, come; dost yer yon bell?
Thou'll ha' yon mill agate   *started*
Afore thou'rt up! Do stir thisel',
Or else thou'll be too late:
I know thou'rt tire't, my lad—I know;
What can a body do?
It's very cowd; but, frost or snow,
Thou knows thou'll ha' to goo!

An' th' north woint's blowin' keen an' shrill;
It's bin a stormy neet;
Thou'll ha' to run o' th' gate to th' mill;   *all the way*
It's thick wi' drivin' sleet;
There's not a candle left i' th' house;
Thou'll don thisel' i' th' dark;
Come, come, my lad; jump up at once,
An' hie tho to thi wark!

I can hardly keep up on my feet;
I'm full o' aches and pains;
An' I's ha' to wesh from morn to neet,   *wash*
For very little gains.
It looks hard fortin' for us both,

86

But it's what we han to dree;   *suffer*
We mun do as weel's we con, my lad;
There's nobbut thee an' me!

Come, come; I have thi stockin's here,
An' thi breeches, an' thi shoon;
Thou'll find thi jacket on yon cheer;
An' thi dinner's upo' th' oon.
I'll lock yon dur, an I'll tak' th' keigh;
I think we's find o' reet;
So manage th' best thou con, my lad,
Till I come whoam at neet!

Then not another word wur said;
But Billy, like a mon,
Geet up out of his little bed,
An' poo'd his stockin's on;
An' off he went, through sleet and snow,
With his dinner in a can;
He'd a bit o' oon-cake in his mouth,   *ovencake*
An' he donned him as he ran.

Some folk can lie till th' clock strikes eight;
Some folk may sleep till ten,
Then rub their e'en an' yawn a bit,
An' turn 'em o'er again;
Some folk can ring a bell i' bed,
Till th' sarvant brings some tay;
But weet or dry, a factory lad
Mun jump at break o' day!

Hard weather
Winter 1878–79   EDWIN WAUGH

Good Lorjus days, what times are these,
For clemmin' an' for cowd;   *going hungry*
For doleful looks, an' wintry nooks,
Where folk are poor an' owd;
For hopeless care an' dark despair,
An' gloomy want o' trust;
For fireless hearths, an' cupboards bare,
An' bitter want o'crust:
But, bide lads bide,
For a happier tide;
An' keep yor hearts out o' yor shoon;

87

Through thick an' thin,
We'n ne'er give in:
There's a bit o' blue sky aboon!

There never wur sich mournful cries
O' famine yerd afore;
John Chinaman's bin clemmed to death,
An' India's suffered sore;
Yor mills may weel be stonnin' still,
Yor markets weel be slack;
For when folk's nipt for want o' meight,
They'n nought to spare for th' back.   *no money to spare
But, bide lads, etc.   for (clothes for) their back*

Sich strikes, an' rows, an' breakages,
There never yet wur known;
Sich frettin', an' sich chettin', an'   *ill-feeling, cheating*
Sich bitter starvin' moan;
These knavish pranks i' trusted banks
Are spreadin' ruin round;
An' every hour, the tradin' ranks
Are crashin' to the ground.
But, bide lads, etc.

Whilst trade declines, an' taxes rise,
And ruin stalks the land,
We groan to see the good we prize,
Crushed by a rampant band;
'Tis ours to watch each bloody fray,
And mad gunpowder plot;
And, win the day whoever may,
'Tis ours to pay the shot.   *bill*
But, bide lads, etc.

Though th' bitter air, an' livin' bare,
Gets keener every day;
An' th' emptier folks' pockets are,
The more they han to pay;
Though strikes, an' wars, an' swindlin' tricks
Are sendin' th' wide world wrong;
Yet, come what will, this shall be still
The burden of my song,—
Bide, lads, bide,
For a happier tide;
An' keep yor hearts out o' yor shoon;
Through thick an' thin,
We'n ne'er give in:
There's a bit o' blue sky aboon!

There's nowt loike spinnin' shoddy

JOSEPH BURGESS

Shoddy, shoddy, shoddy, that's the soart to spin,
There's nowt loike spinnin' shoddy, if yo' want to mak yo'r tin.   *money*
Ne'er moind heaw hard yo' work-un yo'r honds for little wage,   *your workers*
Ther's nowt loike spinnin' shoddy i' this spekilatin' age;
Aber aw would loike to see thoose 'at beigh an' sell sich stuff   *yes, but I*
Start o' spinnin' it thersels, for they'd soon have had enoof,
An' noan be hawve as ready at givin' us ther jaw,   *advice*
Tho' neaw they're loike th' Egyptians when they fun' their slaves   *found*
                              no straw.

Top-clearer laps an' rovin's, under-clearer waste an' fly,
Mak's a very harmless mixin' if they're nobbo' let-un lie,   *left alone*
But, when they're scrutcht an' carded o' purpose to be spun,
It's us poor shoddy piecers as leetun in for th' fun.   *come in for*
Th' ends drop-un deawn loike snow-flakes, whiz upo' th'
                              spindle peint,   *point*
An' we run abeawt an' piece-up till we're crampt i' ev'ry jeint,
Till, if we'd but a minit to do in as we'd loike,
If it wer'n't for bein' laaft at we should sit us deawn an' scroike.

Aw'm a shoddy piecer 'at's singin' yo' this sung,
Bu' tho' aw'm one at present, aw durn't intend 't be lung,
For, ere aw'll stop at piecin', aw'll tell yo' gradely straight,   *keep on*
Aw'll start o' sellin' idleback, an' sheawtin' "weight for weight,"
For what wi' speed an' o'ertoime, an' what wi' dust an' dirt,
Workin' bar'foot upo' th' flooar, i' yo'r breeches an' yo'r shirt,
Fettlin' ev'ry blessed mealtoime four an' five days   *improving machinery*
                              in a week—
If yo' say'n that is no' slav'ry yo'n a toidy lot a' cheek.

An' if aw'm e'er so lucky as to have a little lad,
To coam at neet an' meet me, tak' mi' hont an' co' me "Dad!"
Afore he'st piece on shoddy, an' stew i' th' mill o'day,
Aw'll ax the Gentle Shepherd to tak' His lamb away,
For ere be made a piecer to know what aw have known,
If God 'll nobbo' tak' him aw'st think 'at mercy's shown,
For loife's a deeor bargin when th' price yo' han to pay,
Is piecin' uppo' shoddy for a bob or two a day.

Aw've seen when aw've bin wakkent at foive o'clock i' th' dark,
On bitter frosty mornin's, an' packt off to mi' wark,
An' if, ere th' engine started, aw had no' eylt mi tops,   *not oiled*
Mi moinder 'ud a cusst me, an' cleawted me i' th' chops,   *overseer*

89

An' what wi' th' engine chettin' abeawt ten minits then,   *cheating*
An' runnin' o'er at breakfast toime at leeust another ten,
Wi' seven or eight at six o'clock, an' full fifteen at noon,
It wer' very, very seldom as aw geet theer too soon.

An' when th' reawm's bin so whot aw cud hardly get mi woynt,   *breath*
An' th' spinning's bin so bad 'at aw've piect till welly bloynt,   *almost blind*
If aw'd happent let mi ends deawn an' made a nick or two,
Mi moinder 'ud ha' punst me till aw wer' black an' blue.   *punched*
An' ere a choilt o' moine 'at had striven o' it cud,   *tried as hard as*
To add to th' mesthu's profit by makkin' bad wark good,   *it could*
Should be trayted loike a slave i' freeedom's native isle,
Aw cud lay it in its grave an' feel relievt enoof to smoile.

Why! A fact'ry's loike a prison, yo' con noather see nor yer,
(When yo'n getten once insoide it) owt 'at's passin' eawt o' th' dur,
For they're filled wi' frosted windows, an' built insoide a yard,
Wi' a wall yo' conno' get o'er, an' dur 'at's allus barred.
So aw'm beawn to save mi oddie 'at when aw get upgroon,   *pocket money*
Aw con bid good-bye to shoddy an' to workin' beawt mi shoon,
An' hopin' yo' as yer'n me'll think aw'm doin' reet,
An' clap me leawd an' heartily, aw'll weesh yo' o' good-neet.

A weighver's song   JOHN TRAFFORD CLEGG

Deawn i' th' shed on a summer's day,
Th' owd sun shinin through th' white-weshed top;
Brids on th' slate are chirpin away,
An' aw whistle a tune to every cop;
Clattherin loom an' whirlin wheel,
Flyin' shuttle an' steady reed—
This is wark to make a mon feel
There's wur jobs nor weighvin i' time o' need.   *worse*

Straight-drawn alley an' clen white wo's,
Pickin-pegs noddin their yeads o reaund,
Warps bendin deawn like wayther-fo's,   *waterfalls*
Cog-wheels rattlin a merry seaund,
Tidy skips runnin o'er wi weft,
Snowy cloth windin on to th' byem—   *beam*
Take a good sniff o' th' flyon drift   *dust from cotton*
It's clay an' dust, an' we're nobbut th' same.

Lads an' lasses stonnin i' rows,
Wortchin away fro morn to neet;

90

Tenters—Bobs, Sals, Betty's, an' Joes—
Runnin abeaut o' their nimble feet,
Keepin time to a steady tune
Played bi th' engine fro leet to dark
(Feed him wi wayther an coal, beaut spoon,   *not soft stuff*
An' he's olez reet for another day's wark);

Weighvin cotton o sizes an' maks,
Tablecloths, hanketchers, owts an' nowts,
Shirts for niggers an' 'Merica blacks,
Towels for Chinamen, India clouts,
Dhooties, jacconets, sheetings, twills,
Yard-wide, narrow-width, heavy an' leet,
Brats and pettiicwots, fancies, drills—   *aprons*
We con weighve owt, an' weighve it reet!

Deawn i' th' shed on a winther's day,
Th' sun asleep in his cleaudy bed,
Scores o' gasleets blazin away
On shinin pulley an' snowy thread;
Clattherin loom an' whirlin wheel,
Flyin shuttle an' steady reed—
This is wark to make a mon feel
There's wur jobs nor weighvin i' time o' need.

Hawf past five at neet   WILLIAM BARON

For fooak at's slaves to t' factory bell,
Life's noan so breet nor gay;
For every morn they start at six,
An' wark like foo's o' t' day.   *all day*
Bud when id geds tort stoppin' time,   *toward*
Ther sinkin' hearts grow leet;
An' sich a change comes o'er 'em o,
At hawf past five at neet.

Id meks 'em feel so glad, to know
Ther labour's o'er once mooar;
An' lots o' faces breeten up,
'At looked quite sad befooar.
They swarm like bees throo t' factory gate,
To th' oppen air i' t' street;
An' leeave o' t' cares o' toil behind,
At hawf past five at neet.

Ther's t' chap as fuddled t' neet afooar,   *went drinking*
An' geet aboon his share;
He's ready, soon as th' engine stops,
To dart off like a hare.
Another pint or two, he ses,
Ull mek him feel o' reet;
An' in he pops at t'nearest "pub,"
At hawf past five at neet.

Yo'll see t' young lasses decked i' smiles,
O rushin' fro' ther wark;
To ged donned up to meet ther chaps,
An' ramble reawnd bi t' park.
It's t' thowts o' t' walk, an' t' pleasant talk,
'At meks ther faces breet;
An' fills ther hearts wi' sweet content,
At hawf past five at neet.

For t' chap at's fagged an' wearied eawt,
Wi' t' toil he's done throo t' day;
Id brings a spell o' welcome rest,
To drive o' t' gloom away.
An' when he reyches th' hooam fireside,
Wheer o's so snug an' breet,
He feels 'at life's woth livin' for,
At hawf past five at neet.

It's th' only time as warkin' fooak
Con tek life as they choose;
An' sit an' smook, or ready some book,
Or talk o'er th' latest news.
Or ramble eawt, at t' clooase o' day,
When t' summer air smells sweet;
For slavery's theirs—an nowt no mooar,
Till hawf past five at neet.

To t' sons o' toil, wode'er they be,   *whatever*
Id flings ids joys areawnd;
Id cheers up mony a weary heart,
An' meks ther sperrits beawnd.
Id brings 'em t' tidin's 'at they're free,
An' meks ther burdens leet;
Hey! t' richest gem o' factory life,
Is hawf past five at neet.

Six o'clock at mornin'

WILLIAM BARON

people come out of the factory

When t' factory loces uv a neet,
An' labour's o'er for t'day;
Wod throngs o' warkin' fooak yo'll meet,
Wi' spirits leet an' gay.
Wi' step so brisk, they trip along,
While jibe an' banter, jest and song,
Breyk eawt fro' t' lips o' t' merry throng
When hooam fro' work retornin';
But, wod a wondrous change we see!—
An' mony a time it's puzzled me,
Why things should so much different be
At six o'clock at mornin'.

Yo'll see lots scutter off—pell-mell,
As six o'clock draws near;
While t' warnin' nooates o' t' factory bell,
Ring eawt so bowd an' clear.
While some,—so cheery t' neet afooar,
Wi' faces long, an' hearts so sooar,
Creep siowly to ther wark once mooar,
No smiles ther cheeks adornin';
No sheawts o' laughter seawnd i' th' air,
Ther broo's are dark wi' cleawds o' care,
For life seems like a desert bare,
At six o'clock at mornin'.

Ther's t' young chap theer 'at cuts a dash,
An' dons up every neet;
He's short o' nowt but brains an' cash,
For he's plenty o' conceit.
Wi' t' billiard cue he's quite a don,
Gets tumblin' drunk,—to be a mon,
An' soo i' vice he rushes on,
Nor every thinks o' tornin';
His blook-shot een, an' features pale,
His limbs 'at strength begins to fail,
They tell a sad an' weary tale,
At six o'clock at mornin'.

Yo'll see some odd 'uns, rayther late,
Come pushin' on ther way;
They hurry deawn tort t' factory gate,
Wi' feelin's far fro gay.
They're past ther time,—they feel quite sure,
An' as they enter t' watch-heawse dooar,

They hear ther tackler rave an' rooar,—   *foreman*
Ther wild excuses scornin';
An' then as to ther looms they run,
They find 'at somebry's set 'em on,
An' med a greyt big 'mash i' one,   *flaw*
At six o' clock at mornin'.

An' sooa they peyl along o' day,   *get along*
Till neet comes on ageean;
But o' ther troubles fly away,
When freed fro' labour's cheean.   *chain*
It's quite a study, aw declare,
To watch heaw th' humbler classes fare,
O' t' toil an' strife they hev ther share,
As t' wheel o' life keeps tornin';
Tho' factory life's weel mixed wi' woe,
Yo'll find id mixed wi' joys an' o,
But t' biggest drawbeck uv id o,
Is—six o'clock at mornin'.

Strike song   MARY THOMASON

Come, Mary, put mi pit clogs by,
From th' jacket shake the dust,
We've gone on strike for ten per cent;
We'll get it lass, I trust.
Ther's nothing cheers a house so much
As a bright fire o' coal,
Yet colliers' wages scarce will keep
The body with the soul.

But we're on strike for ten per cent,
We're not downhearted yet,
We are on strike for ten per cent,
And ten per cent we'll get.

Don't bother much o'er food for me,
But give eawr Joe enough.
If he and thee get decent meals,
I will put up with rough.
And cheer thee up, mi bonnie lass,
And little Joe, don't fret,
That dobbie-horse I promised thee,
When th' strike is o'er theay'll get.

For we're on strike for ten per cent,
We're not downhearted yet,
We are on strike for ten per cent,
And ten per cent we'll get.

Hard times

H. B. WHITEHEAD

Yoh munnut come agen hard times;
We thowt thoose days were done,
When th' dust lay thick i' th' jinny-gate,   *alley*
Where the wheels no longer run;
When th' yed-stocks stood like silent ghosts,   *head-stocks*
And th' straps and ropes were still;
Where o abeawt 'em seemed to say,
"There's nowt to do it th' mill."

Yoh munnut come agen hard times,
For Owdham's had its share.
When th' purse were thin, and times were bad,
And ther' weren't mich to spare;
When nob'dy axed, or seemed to care,
Heaw were its troubles met?
Thoose wounds lie deep, the scars remain,
The folk remember yet.

Yoh munnut come to haunt these streets,
Where once yoh left your mark;
Where care and want together walked,
Wi' thousands eawt o' wark;
Where daycent men, fro' daycent whoms,
Wi' brocken heart and soul,
Went trudgin' deawn that hopeless road,
To th' means test and the dole.

The Cotton Panic

Th' Surat weyver WILLIAM BILLINGTON

We're werkin lads frae Lankisheer,
Un gradely daysent fooak;
We'n hunted weyvin far un near,
Un could'nd ged a strooak;
We'n sowd booath table, clock un cheer,
Un popt booath shoon un hat, *pawned*
Un borne wod mortal mon could bear,
Affoor we'd wevye Surat!

Ids neeah aboon a twelmon gone *now more than a year*
Sin t' Yankee war brooake eeat;
Un t' poor's traade herd to potter on *tried hard to get along*
Tell t' rich ud potter eeat; *pay out*
We'n left no stooan unturn'd, nod one, *not one*
Sin t' trade becoom so flatt,
Bud neeah they'n browt us to id, mon,
They'n *med* us wevye Surat! *made*

Aw've yerd fooak toke o' t' treydin mill,
Un pickin' oakum too;
Bud stransportashun's nod as ill
As weyvin rotton Su!
Ids bin too monny for yar Bill, *too much*
Un aw'm as thin as a latt, *a lath*
Bud uv wey wi t' Yankees hed ur will, *if we had our way with*
We'd hang em i' t' Surat! *the Yankees*

Ids just laake rowlin stooans up t' broo, *hill*
Or twistin rooaps o' sand;—
Yo piece yore twist, id comes i' two,
Laake copwebs i' yor hand;
Aw've werk'd un woven laake a foo!
Tell aw'm as weak as a cat,
Yet after o as aw could do
Aw'm konkurd bi t' Surat!

Yar Mally's i' t' twist fever, un
Meh feyther's getten begg'd; *sacked*
Strenge tecklers win nod teck him on, *foremen*
Becose his cooat's so ragg'd!
Me moother ses ids welly done— *nearly*
Hoo'l petch id wi her brat, *patch it with her apron*
Un meck id fit for ony mon
Whod roots among t' Surat!

Aw wonst imagund Deeoth's a very   *once*
Dark un dismal face;
Bud neeah aw fancy t' cemetery
Is quaate a pleasant place!
Bud sin wey took yar Bill to bury,
Aw've offen wish'd Owd Scrat   *the Devil*
Ud fotch o t' bag-o-tricks un lorry, *bring all his helpers and drag*
To hell wi o' t' Surat!

The Shurat weaver's song SAMUEL LAYCOCK

Confound it! aw ne'er wur so woven afore,
Mi back's welly brocken, mi fingers are sore;
Aw've bin starin' an' rootin' amung this Shurat,
Till aw'm very near getten as bloint as a bat.

Every toime aw go in wi' mi cuts to owd Joe,
He gies mi a cursin', an' bates mi an' o; *keeps back part of payment*
Aw've a warp i' one loom wi' booath selvedges marr'd
An' th' other's as bad, for he's dressed it to' hard.

Aw wish aw wur fur enough off, eawt o' th' road,
For o' weavin' this rubbitch aw'm gettin' reet stow'd; *fed up*
Aw've nowt i' this world to lie deawn on but straw,
For aw've nobbut eight shillin' this fortn't to draw.

Neaw aw haven't mi family under mi hat,
Aw've a woife an' six childer to keep eawt o' that;
So aw'm rayther amung it at present, yo' see,
Iv ever a fellow wur puzzl't, it's me!

Iv one turns eawt to stale, folk 'll co me a thief, *steal*
An' aw conno' put th' cheek on to ax for relief;
As aw said i' eawr heawse t' other neet to mi woife,
Aw never did nowt o' this sort i' mi loife.

One doesn't like everyone t' know heaw they are,
But we'n suffered so lung thro' this 'Merica war,
'At ther's lots o' poor factory folk getten t' fur end,
An' they'll soon be knocked o'er iv th' toimes dunno mend.

Oh, dear! iv yon Yankees could only just see
Heaw they're clemmin' an starvin' poor weavers loike me,
Aw think they'd soon settle the'r bother, an' strive
To send us some cotton to keep us alive.

Ther's theawsands o' folk just i' th' best o' the'r days,
Wi' traces o' want plainly seen i' the'r face;
An' a future afore 'em as dreary an' dark,
For when th' cotton gets done we shall o' be beawt wark. *all be without work*

We'n bin patient an' quiet as lung as we con;
Th' bits o' things we had by us are welly o gone; *almost all gone*
Aw've bin trampin' so lung, mi owd shoon are worn eawt,
An' mi halliday clooas are o on 'em "up th' speawt." *pawned*

It wur nobbut last Monday aw sowd a good bed—
Nay, very near gan it—to get us some bread; *gave*
Afore these bad toimes come aw used to be fat,
But neaw, bless yo'r loife, aw'm as thin as a lat!

Mony a toime i' mi loife aw'v seen things lookin' feaw, *ugly*
But never as awk'ard as what they are neaw;
Iv ther' isn't some help for us factory folk soon,
Aw'm sure we shall o be knocked reet eawt o' tune.

Come, give us a lift, yo' 'at han owt to give,
An' help yo'r poor brothers an' sisters to live;
Be kind, an' be tender to th' needy an' poor,
An' we'll promise when th' toimes mend we'll ax yo' no moor.

Philip Clough's tale   JOSEPH RAMSBOTTOM

Eh! dear! what weary toimes are these,
There's nob'dy ever knew 'em wur; *worse*
For honest wortchin' folk one sees
By scores reawnd th' Poor-law office dur.
It's bad to see 't, bo wus a dyeal, *a good deal worse*
Wen one's sel helps to mak up th' lot;
We'n nowt to do, we darno steyle
Nor con we beighl an empty pot *boil*

Aw hate this pooin' oakum wark,
An' breakin' stones to get relief;
To be a pauper—pity's mark—
Ull break an honest heart wi grief.
We're mixt wi th' stondin paupers too, *permanent*
Ut winno wortch' when wark's t' be had; *won't work*
Con this be reet for them to do,
To tak no thowt o' good or bad?

To wortch wi' paupers aw'd noa do 't,
Aw'd starve until aw sunk to th' floore;
Bo th' little childher bring me to 't—
One's like to bend for them, yo're sure.
Heawever hard things are or queer,
We're loike to tak 'em as they come;
For th' cravin' stomach's awlus theer,
An' childer conno clem awhoam.   *starve at home*

When wark fell off aw did mi best
To keep misel an' fam'ly clear;
Mi wants aw've never forrud prest,
For pity is a thing to fear.
Mi little savin's soon wur done,
An' then aw sowd mi toothri things—   *two or three*
Mi books an' bookcase o are gone,—
Mi mother's picther, too, fun wings.

A bacco box wi two queer lids,
Sent whoam fro' Indy by John Bell;
Mi fuschia plants an' pots, mi brids
An' cages too, aw're forced to sell.
Mi feyther's rockin' cheer's gone,
Mi mother's corner cubbart, too;
An' th' eight days clock has followed, mon;
What con a hongry body do?

Aw've gan mi little garden up,
Wi' mony a pratty fleawr an' root;
Aw've sowd mi gronny's silver cup,
Aw've sowd mi uncle Robin's flute;
Aw've sowd mi tables, sowd mi beds,
Mi bedstocks, blankets, sheets as weel;   *mattresses*
Oitch neet o' sthraw we rest eawr yeads,
An' we an' God known what we feel.

Aw've sowd until aw've nowt to sell,
An' heaw we'n clemm'd 's past o' belief;
An' wheer to geo aw couldno tell,
Except to th' "Booard" to get relief.
Ther wur no wark, for th' mill wur stopt;
Mi childher couldno dee, yo known:
Aw'm neaw a pauper, cose aw've dhropt
To this low state o' breakin' stone.

Bo once aw knew a diff'rent day,
When ev'ry heawr ud comfort bring;

Aw earn'd mi bread an' paid mi way,—
Aw wouldno stoop to lord or king.
Aw felt mi independence then,
Mi sad dependance neaw aw know;
Shall e'er aw taste thoose jeighs agen,   *joys*
Or e'er live thro' these days o' woe?

Th' owd pedlar   JOSEPH RAMSBOTTOM

Well, want yo pins or neelds today,
Or buttons, threed, or hooks an' eyes?
Or want yo tape or petch-wark, pray,
Or stockins, good an' chep,—your size?
What? not today! Well, thoose mun pass;
Bo is ther nowt yo met ha' had?
Here, beigh a doll for th' little lass,
Or marbles—come—for th' little lad.

He's flertin' yon i th' loane, aw see,   *flicking with his finger*
His taw's too big by mony a bit;
This alley 'll shute him to a tee,
An' noa be hauve as yesy t' hit!   *easy*
Yo han no thrade. Well, then, good day!
Heaw hard th' toimes are! Aw tell yo whot
Sin folks han bin too poor to pay,
This counthry side's an autthert spot.   *altered*

Aw've fun it so: it's noan long sin   *found*
Ut folks ud sheawt shus wheer aw went,—   *everywhere*
"Well, Bob, what hasto fresh?—come in!"
An' lots o' brass they awlus spent.
Bo some at th' dur ull meet me neaw,
An' some ull come to th' top o' th' fowt;   *village*
Mi prattiest things they co'n em feaw,   *ugly*
Or quietly sen they're wantin' nowt.

Aw know their dhrift—aw see it o':
They conno mak' things t' square an' fit;
Oitch thries t' noa let his neighbour know
Heaw fast he's wastin', bit by bit.   *getting poorer*
Bo folks mun sthrive to do ther part,
Tho' Want an' Sorrow in the breast
May nestlin' gnaw, an' at the heart
Still gnaw an' suck, an' never rest.

102

Neaw ev'ry cheek has lost its rose,
Its bwons are creepin' eawt to th' leet;   *bones*
Wi starin' een, an' sharpent nose,
An' sallow face,—it's sad to see 't.
When ev'ry whoam is nak'd an' bare,
Folks conno beigh, bo aw con tell,
Ut pedlar Bob comes in for th' share,
O th' hardships, neaw he conno sell.

Ther's nob'dy want a ribbin neaw,
Ther's nob'dy wants mi fancy rings;
They're o' too poor, aw weel know heaw
It is they dunno beigh my things.
For sunken cheeks, and starin' een
Ud match bo ill a weel dhress'd yead;   *would be a bad match for*
An' one ne'er thinks o' dhress, yo seen,
When th' stomach's skroikin' eawt for bread.

Folks are ill off, an' ill they look,
An' aw'm as ill as them, for sure,
Mi palsied wife, hoo sits i' th' nook,
Mi cripplet dowther plays o' th' floore.
Eawr Jack's a sailor, off at th' sae,
Eawr Nanny neaw just jobs abeawt,   *does odd jobs*
Aw do a bit i' th' peddlin' way,
When th' rheumatiz ull let me eawt.

An' mony a time we're hardly set,   *in great difficulty*
Sthrive heaw we win, do what we con;   *will*
It fairly makes one t' fume an' fret,
Sich wark to get a torin' on.   *meagre living by*
Ther's little jeigh i' th' poor mon's part,
When thrials come i' sich a shoal;
They choke the sweet springs of the heart,
The kindlier nature of the soul.

Neaw th' winter's past and spring is green,
Fleawr's laugh at me an' peighnt to th' sky—   *point*
Aw conno laugh at them, yo seen,
My laugh ud be bo mockery.
Aw'm writhin' under th' weight o' grief
Ut long has prest me close to th' sod;
That dyeth may soon bring sweet relief   *death*
Is o' mi yearnsful prayer to God.   *earnest*

It's hard to ceawer i' th' chimney nook

SAMUEL LAYCOCK

It's hard to ceawer i' th' chimney nook,
Fro' weary day to day;
An' no kind word, nor lovin' look
To drive one's care away!
Mi clooas are welly o worn eawt,
An' neaw aw'm sich a seet,
Aw dunno' loike to walk abeawt
Unless it's dark at neet.

To get us bread, mi mother sowd
Eawr mattrasses an' sheets;
An' oh! it is so bitter cowd,
These frosty winter neets!
Two ladies kindly co'd one day,
An' put us deawn some shoon;   *shoes*
They said they'd sheets to give away,
An' we must ha' some soon.

Eawr Mary Jane's a bonny lass,
Wi' two such rosy cheeks;
Hoo goes to th' Refuge sewin' class,
An' has done neaw for weeks.
Poor thing! hoo's badly starved, aw know,   *very cold*
Hoo's scarcely owt to wear;
Aw do so wish 'at somebody'd co,
'At's getten owt to spare.

Her petticoats are o worn eawt;
Her Sunday frock's i' holes;
An' then her boots—hoos's welly beawt—   *almost without*
They want booath heels an' soles.
Aw wish mi feyther had a job,
He looks so strange an' wild;
He'll sit for heawers at th' side o' th' hob,
An' cry just like a child.

No wonder he should pine an' fret,
An' look soa discontent;
For th' gas bill isn't settled yet,
An' th' lon'lord wants his rent.
Mi mother's bin to th' shop toneet,
To fetch a bit o' tay;
Hoo says they hardly looken reet,   *looked pleasant*
Becose hoo conno pay.

An' who con blame 'em? Nob'dy con;
They're wur nor us, bi th' mass!
Iv they're to pay for what they han,
They're loike to ha' some brass;   *must have*
We'n lived as careful as we con
Aw'm sure, but after o
A great big shop score's runnin' on,
For twothry pewnd or so.   *two or three*

Aw've etten bacon till aw'm sick;
Eawr Jimmy has an' o;
An' iv yo'll ax mi uncle Dick,
He'll tell yo' th' same, aw know.
Of porritch aw've had quite enoo,
For they dunno suit, aw find;
Aw conno do wi' soup an' stew,
They fill one full o' wind.

Aw'm glad o' every bit aw get,
An' rare an' thankful feel;
Aw've allus getten summat yet,
To mak' misel a meal.
Thank God! we'n never ax'd i' vain,
For folk are kind, aw'm sure;
God bless 'em o for what they'n gan;   *given*
One conno say no moor.

Frettin'   JOSEPH RAMSBOTTOM

Fro heawrs to days—a dhreary length—
Fro days to weeks, one idle stonds,
An' slowly sinks fro pride an' sthrength,
To weeny heart an' wakely honds.   *small heart and feeble hands*
An' still one hopes, an' ever thries
To think ut betther days mun come;
Bo th' sun may set, an' th' sun may rise,
No sthreak o' leet we find awhoam.

When o' above wur blue an' breet,
An' o' below, wur sweet an' fair,
Aw've sat o' th' harstone mony a neet,   *hearthstone*
An' plans for th' future built i' th' air.
To th' future neaw aw durno look,
Wi growin' ills it is so dark;
Mi castle buildin' neaw i' th' nook
Runs back to th' days when aw'r i' wark.   *in work*

105

Aw want to see thoose days agen,
To see folks earn what e'er they need;
O God, to think ut wortchin' men
Should be poor things to pet an' feed!
Ther's some to th' bastile han to goo,   *workhouse*
To live o' th' rates they'n help'd to pay;
An' some get dow to help em thro',   *dole*
An' some are ta'en or sent away.

An' private pets some are like me,
O' folks ut watch o'er what they give;
Ut oather send or come to see
What mwost we need ut we may live.
An' o' is theirs shushwheer we look,   *everywhere*
Aye, deawn to th' twothri things one wears;
An' th' feighr to warm th' owd heawse, an' cook,
An' even th' mayt we eat is theirs.

We tak whate'er they han to give,
Wi thankful heart an' oppen hond;
An' this is th' road we han to live,
Poor propt up things ut conno stond.
An' to an' fro one walks i' th' loane,
Fro th' break o'day far into th' dark,
Wi' mony a soik an' mony a moan,   *sigh*
An' heart-sick longin' afther wark.

An' bent wi o' these heavy sthrokes
We hang eawr yeads when eawt i' th' leet,
An' this depending uppo folks
Oft makes us blush i' th' dark o' th' neet.
Day afther day wi nowt to do
Bo int' eawr deep'nin' sthrem o' care,   *stream*
Keep wadin' fur, ne'er gettin' thro',   *further*
Ull stifle hope an' breed despair.

Whot is ther here ut one should live,
Or wish to live, weigh'd deawn wi' grief,
Thro' weary weeks and months, ut give
Not one short heawr o' sweet relief?
A sudden plunge, a little blow
At once ud eend mi care an' pain!
An' why noa do 't?—for weel aw know
Aw lose bo ills, if nowt aw gain.   *only*

Aye, why noa do 't?—it ill ud tell   *effect badly*
O' thoose wur left beheend, aw fear:

It's wrong at fust to kill mysel,
An' wrong to lyev mi childer here.
One's like to tak some thowt for them—   *must take thought*
Some sort o' comfort one should give;
So one mun bear, an' starve, an' clem,   *go cold and hungry*
An' pine, an' mope, an' fret, an' live.

Aw've turned mi bit o' garden o'er

SAMUEL LAYCOCK

Aw've turned mi bit o' garden o'er,
An' set mi seed an' o;
Soa neaw aw've done, aw'll rest a bit,
An' sit an' watch it grow.
It's noice to have a little spot,
Wheer one can ceawer 'em down,
A quiet comfortable place,
Eawtside o' th' busy teawn,
Wheer one can sit an' smoke the'r poipe,
An' have a friendly chat,
Or read th' newspapper o'er a bit,
Or talk abeawt Shurat;
Or listen to some owd mon's tale,
Some vet'ran come fro' th' wars;
Aw loike to yer 'em spin the'r yarn,
An' show the'r wounds an' scars.

One neet aw thowt aw'd tak' a walk
As far as th' Hunter's Teawer,
To beg a daisy root or two:
Tom's gan me mony a fleawer.   *given*
They're bloomin' i' mi garden neaw,
Aw've sich a bonny show;
Aw've daisies, pinks, carnations, too,
An' pollyants an' o.
Yo' couldn't think heaw preawd aw feel,
O' every plant an' fleawer;
Aw couldn't ha' cared for childer moor,
Aw've nursed 'em mony a heawer.   *hour*
But tho' they neaw look fresh an' fair,
They'll droop the'r yeads an' dee;
They hanno lung to tarry here,
They're just loike yo' an' me.

Dark-lookin' cleawds are gatherin' reawnd,
Aw think it's beawn to rain;
Ther's nowt could pleos me better neaw,
Aw should be rare and fain!
Mi bit o' seed wants deggin' o'er,   *sprinkling over*
To help to mak' it spreawt;
It's summat loike a choild's first teeth,
'At wanten helpin' eawt.
But aw'll be off, afore aw'm wet,
It's getten reet agate;   *started properly*
An' while it comes aw think aw'll get
A bit o' summat t' ate;
For, oh, it is a hungry job,
This workin' eawt o' th' door;
Th' committee should alleaw for this,
An' give one rayther moor.

Aw should so loike a good blow eawt,   *big meal*
A feed off beefsteak pie;
But aw can ne'er get nowt loike that
Wi' th' bit aw draw, not I!
Aw'm glad enough o' porritch neaw,
Or tothrey cold potates;   *two or three*
Iv aw can get enoo o' these,
Aw'st do till th' factory gates.   *manage till the factory starts again*
It's welly gan o'er rainin', so
Aw'll have another look,
An' see heaw th' gardens's gettin on;
An' then aw'll get a book,
An' read an heawer or two for th' woife,
An' sing a bit for Ted;
Then poo mi clogs off, fasten th' doors,
An' walk upsteers to bed.

Eawr factory skoo   E. MOSS

Ther never wur such times as these, naw, nee'r sin th' world wur made,
Ther's nowt but gents un ladies neaw, ut's work'd i' th' cotton trade,
For harder toimes wur never felt, that's weel known to be true,
Un th' hardest wark we han just neaw, is gooin to th' Factory Skoo.
    Chorus
    We're ladies neaw un gentlemen,
    Un paid for gooin Skoo.

108

Six heawrs a day we han th' be there. furt make us
                                    o moor wise,   *to make us all*
One heawr ther is for reedin, un one heawr for exercise,
For sodiers soon we shall o be, bekose we'n nowt else th' do,
To guard eawr whoms un country, eawr Queen, un th' Factory Skoo.

Some lads ith' little spellin reads, un some does rule o' three,
Un some uts gone to th eend o' th' book, are a good deol fur nor me; *further*
Ther's others if they getten th' news, ul read for one or two,   *newspaper*
Un tawk of war, distress, or trade, at eawr Factory Skoo.

Un th' women too are larnin sew, un larnin rite and reed,
They'r makin shirts un neetcaps, un other things we need,
When th' panic's o' er they'll mak good wives, un ne'er ha' cause to rue,
They'll bless an praise thoose panic days, they went to th' Factory Skoo.

It's a trate these times th' see owd un yung, attendin to ther books, *treat*
No heavy troubles weighs um deawn, to judge um by ther looks,
Un very kind it is to o' ut helps us th' winter throo,
We'n return it back a theawsand toimes o th'
                                    breaking up ut Skoo.   *when the school finishes*

Eawr pashunce and eawr fortitude, is known throo eawt the world,
Un th' banner with the word "Distress" is everywhere unfurl'd,
Let Yankees raise ther flag o' peace, un bid God speed the plough,
We'll shew um then i' England whot we larnt at th' Factory Skoo.

Sewin' class song   SAMUEL LAYCOCK

Come, lasses, let's cheer up, an' sing, it's no use lookin' sad,
We'll mak' eawr sewin' schoo' to ring, an' stitch away loike mad;
We'll mak' th' best job we con o' owt we han to do,
We read an' write, an' spell an' kest, while here at th' sewin' schoo'.   *add up*
    Chorus
        Then, lasses, let's cheer up an' sing, etc.

Eawr Queen, th' Lord Mayor o' London, too, they send us lots o' brass,
An' neaw, at welly every schoo', we'n got a sewin' class;
We'n superintendents, cutters eawt, an' visitors an' o;   *cutters out*
We'n parsons, cotton mesturs, too, come in to watch us sew.

Sin' th' war begun, an' th' factories stopped, we're badly off, it's true.
But still we needn't grumble, for we'n noan so mich to do;
We're only here fro' nine to four, an' han an heawer for noon.
We noather stop so very late nor start so very soon.

It's noice an' easy sittin' here, ther's no mistake i' that,
We'd sooner do it, a foine seet, nor root amung th' Shurat;   *a good deal*
We'n ne'er floats to unweave neaw, we're reet enough, bi th' mass,   *faults*
For we couldn't have an easier job nor goin' to th' sewin' class.

We're welly killed wi' kindness neaw, we really are, indeed,
For everybody's tryin' hard to get us o we need;
They'n sent us puddins, bacon, too, an' lots o' dacent cloes,
An' what they'll send afore they'n done ther's nob'dy here 'at knows.

God bless these kind, good-natured folk, 'at sends us o this stuff,
We conno tell 'em o we feel, nor thank 'em hawve enough;
They help to find us meat an' clooas, an' eddicashun, too,
An' what creawns o, they give us wage for goin' to th' sewin' schoo'.

We'n sich a chance o' larnin' neaw we'n never had afore:
An' oh, we shall be rare an' wise when th' Yankee wars are o'er;
Ther's nob'dy then con puzzle us wi' owt we'n larned to do,
We'n getten polished up so weel wi' goin' to th' sewin' schoo'

Young fellows lookin' partners eawt had better come this way,
For neaw we'n larned to mak' a shirt, we're ready ony day;
But mind, they'll ha' to ax us twice, an' mak' a deol ado,   *make a great effort*
We're gettin' rayther saucy neaw, wi' goin' to th' sewin' schoo'.

Ther'll be some lookin' eawt for wives when th' factories start ogen,   *again*
But we shall never court wi' noan but dacent, sober men;
So vulgar chaps, beawt common sense, will ha' no need to come,
For sooner nur wed sich as these, we'd better stop a-whoam.

Come lasses, then, cheer up an' sing, it's no use lookin' sad,
We'll mak' eawr sewin' schoo' to ring, an' stitch away loike mad;
We live i' hopes afore so lung, to see a breeter day,
For th' cleawd 'at's hangin' o'er us neaw is sure to blow away.
        Chorus
        Then, Lasses, let's cheer up an' sing, etc.

Gooin' t' schoo   JOSEPH RAMSBOTTOM

Heaw slow these weary weeks dhrag on,
Th' hard toimes ull ne'er be o'er, aw'm sure;
Eawr mill's bin stondin' idle yon
For these last eighteen months, or mooar.
We walk abeawt i' th' leet o' th' day
I' clooas ut sumdy else has bowt;

Think o'er it when an' heaw we may,
We're like to own it's up to nowt. *must admit it's no good*

To thrust to sumdy else for bread, *trust*
An' by th' relief keep torin' on, *making a meagre living*
Maks honest folk to hang their yead,
An' crushes th' heart o' th' preawdest mon.
We known it's not eawr bread we ate,
We known they're not eawr clooas we wear,
We want agen eawr former state,
Eawr former dhrudgin' life o' care.

Toime wur, if amdy dust ha worn, *anybody*
Sich things as neaw are worn by me,
Ut folks ud sheawt wi jeers an' scorn,
"Eh! thoose are 'thank yo, sirs', aw see."
Bo sheawts and jeers like these are o'er,
Neaw nob'dy's reawm to mak a stir;
If wortchin' folk yo meet by th' score, *working*
Oitch one ull wear a "thank yo, sir."

It's fro no faut o eawrs, it's true,
An' folks han met eawr wants like men,
Like brothers an' like sisters too,—
May th' great God pay em back agen.
Heawe'er aw grumble at mi state,
Aw've no hard word to say to them;
Aw thank the poor, aw thank the great,
Ut couldno stond to see us clem. *starve*

Their help has bin great help to me,
It's that alone ut sent me t' schoo;
It's that ut towt me th' A B C,
For o aw'd turnt o' forty-two. *although I was*
'T wur rayther hard at fust to sit
An' stare at things aw couldno tell,
Cose when owt puzzl't me a bit,
O th' lads ud laugh among thersel'.

A mon grown up, an' owd as me,
To stop before a letther fast; *stuck*
Wur gradely fun for them to see,
Bo aw geet thro', an' that's o' past.
I' th' news aw neaw con read a bit;
I' the' Bible spell a chapther thro';
Con write a line ut's fair an' fit;
An' multiply, divide, an' do.

On lots o' things aw get new leet,
Mi idle toime's noan badly spent;
To th' wife an' th' childher neaw oitch neet
Aw read a bit i' th' Testiment,
Heaw Jesus Christ once fed the poor,
An' th' little childher to him co'd;
Heaw th' sick an' blind he oft did cure,
An' th' lame to help 'em on their road.

When o' these weary toimes are past—
When th' schoos an' o' are past away—
These happy neets awhoam ull last,
At th' eend o'mony a breetther day:— *brighter*
Bo th' eend o' th' ill it's hard to see,
An' very hard to battle thro';
A gradely plague it's bin to me—
It's bin a gradely blessin' too.

Aw wod this war
wur ended   WILLIAM BILLINGTON

There's nobuddy knows wod we'n gooan through
Sin' th' factories stopt at fost,   *first*
An' heaw mitch life's bin wasted too,
An' heaw mitch brass we'n lost;
Aw trys sometimes to reckon up,
Bud keawntin connud mend id;
When aw sit deawn wi nowt to sup—
Aw wod this war wur ended.   *wish*

A boddy's lifetime's nod so lung—
Nod them as lives to th' lungest;
Sooa dusend id seem sadly wrung
For th' healthiest an' strungest
To give three wul years' pith an' pride   *whole*
To rust an' ruin blended,
An' ravin up o' th' loss beside?—   *taking up*
Aw wod this war wur ended!

A dacent chap ull do his best,
An' eawt o' wod he's earnin'
Ged th' owdest son a trade, an' th' rest
O' th' lads a bit o' learnin';

112

Bud iv he's eawt o' wark; wey then,
Unschollard, unbefriended,
His childer grow up into men—
Aw wod this war wur ended!

As times has bin, aw owt some "tin"   *owed some money*
For shop stuff ut Lung Nailey's,
An' cose aw cuddent pay't, yo sin,
He's gooan an' sent th' bum bailies;
They'n sowd us up, booath pot an' pooak,   *bag*
An' paid th' owd scoor off splendid;
They just dun wod they will wi fooak.—
Aw wod this war wur ended.

Neaw aw feer noather dun nor bum,
Wi o their kith an' kin—
They'll fotch nowt eawt o' th' heawse, by gum!
Becose there's nowt left in;
Aw'm welly weary o' mi life,
An' cuddend, if aw'd spend id,
Ged scran for th' kids, mysel', an' th' wife.—   *food*
Aw wod this war wur ended!

Some forrud foos rant reet hard,   *forward fools*
An' toke a deal o' nonsense;
Bud let um gabble tell theyr terd,   *tired*
Id's reet enuff i' one sense;
They waste their brass an' rack their brains,
Yet, be nod yo offended,
They'll ged their labour for their pains,
Bud th' war's nod theerby ended!

Some factory maisters tokes for t' Seawth
Wi' a smooth an' oily tongue,
Bud iv they'd sense they'd shut their meawth,
Or sing another song;
Let liberty nod slavery
Be fostered an' extended—
Four million slaves mun yet be free,
An', then t' war will be ended.

Old age

Owd Roddle

EDWIN WAUGH

Owd Roddle wur tattert an' torn,
With a bleart an' geawly e'e;   *rheumy eye*
He're wamble, an' slamp, an' unshorn;   *shaky, and thin, and long-haired*
A flaysome cowt to see: *frightening animal*
Houseless, without a friend,
The poor owd wandrin slave
Crawled on to his journey's end,
Wi' one of his feet i' th' grave!
Poor owd Roddle!

Owd Roddle wur fond of ale,
Fro' tap to tap went he;
An' this wur his endless tale,
"Who'll ston a gill for me?"
He crept into drinkin'-shops
At dawnin' o' mornin' leet;
He lived upo' barmy slops,
An' slept in a tub at neet:
Poor owd Roddle!

As Roddle one mornin'-tide
Wur trailin' his limbs to town,
A twinkle i' th' slutch he spied,
"Egad, it's a silver crown!"
"Now, Roddle, go buy a shirt—
A shirt an' a pair o' shoon!"
"A fig for yor shoon an' shirts;
My throttle's as dry's a oon!"   *oven*
Poor owd Roddle!

"Come, bring us a weel-filled quart;
I connot abide a tot;
Today I've a chance to start
With a foamin', full-groon pot!
This crown has a jovial look;
I'm fleyed it'll melt too fast;   *afraid*
But I'll live like a king i' th' nook
As long as my crown 'll last!"
Poor owd Roddle!

But he met with a friendly touch
That ended his mortal woes;
For he fell in a fatal clutch,
That turned up his weary toes:
Though they missed him i' nooks o' th' town

Where peniless topers meet,
Nob'dy knew how he'd broken down,
Nor where he'd crept out o' seet:
Poor owd Roddle!

In a churchyard corner lone,
Under a nameless mound,
Where the friendless poor are thrown,
Roddle lies sleepin' sound:
And the kind moon shines at night
On the weary wanderer's bed,
And the sun and the rain keep bright
His grassy quilt o'erhead.
Poor owd Roddle!

Owd Enoch   EDWIN WAUGH

Owd Enoch o' Dan's laid his pipe deawn o' th' hob,
And his thin fingers played i' th' white thatch of his nob;
"I'm gettin' done up," to their Betty he said;
"Dost think thae could doff me, an' dad me to bed?"   *undress   lead*
　　Derry down

Then hoo geet him to bed, an' hoo happed him up weel,   *covered well*
An' hoo said to him, "Enoch, lad; heaw doesto feel?"
"These limbs o' mine, Betty,—they're cranky an' sore;   *rusty*
It's time to shut up when one's getten four score."

As hoo potter't abeawt his poor winterly pate,
Th' owd crayter looked dreawsily up at his mate,—
"There's nought on me laft, lass,—do o 'at tho' con,—   *do everything*
But th' cratchinly frame o' what once wur a mon."   *feeble*

Then he turn't hissel' o'er, like a chylt tir't wi' play,
An' Betty crept reawnd, while he're dozin' away;
As his e'e-lids sank deawn, th' owd lad mutter't "Well done!
I think there's a bit o'seawnd sleep comin' on."

Then hoo thought hoo'd sit by till he'd had his nap o'er,—
If hoo'd sit theer till then, hoo'd ha' risen no more;
For he cool't eawt o'th world, an' his e'en lost their leet,
Like a cinder i'th fire-grate i' th' deeod time o' th' neet.

As Betty sit rockin' bith' side of his bed,
Hoo looked neaw an' then at owd Enoch's white yed;
An' hoo thought to hersel' that hoo'd not lung to stay
Iv ever th'owd prop of her life should give way.

117

Then, wondrin' to see him so seawnd an' so still,
Hoo touched Enoch's hond,—an' hoo fund it wur chill;
Says Betty, "He's cowd; I'll put summat moor on!"
But o' wur no use, for Owd Enoch wur gone!

An' when they put Enoch to bed deawn i' th' greawnd,
A rook o' poor neighbours stoode bare-yedded reawnd,   *crowd*
They dropt sprigs o' rosemary: an' this wur their text:—
"Th' owd crayter's laid by,—we may haply be th' next!"

So, Betty wur left to toar on bi hersel';   *make a hard living*
An' heaw hoo poo'd through it no mortal can tell:
But th' doctor dropt in to look at her one day,
When hoo're rockin' bith' side of an odd cup o' tay.

"Well, Betty," said th' doctor, "heaw dun yo get on?
I'm soory to yer 'at yo'n lost yo'r owd mon:
What complaint had he, Betty?" Says hoo, "I caun't tell,
We ne'er had no doctor; he deed of hissel."

"Ay, Betty," said th' doctor; "there's one thing quite sure;
Owd age is a thing that no physic can cure:
Fate will have her way, lass,—do o' that we con,—
When th' time's up, we's ha' to sign o'er, an' be gone."

"Both winter and summer th' owd mower's at wark,
Sidin' folk eawt o' seet, both bi dayleet an' dark!   *moving*
He's slavin' away while we're snorin' i' bed;
An' he'd slash at a king, if it coom in his yed".

"These sodiurs, an' parsons, an' maisters o' lond,
He lays 'em i' th' greawnd, wi' their meawths full o' sond,   *sand*
Rags or riches, an owd greasy cap, or a creawn—
He sarves o' alike,—for he switches 'em deawn."

"The mon that's larnt up, an' the mon that's a foo—   *educated*
It mays little odds, for they both han to goo;
When they com'n within th' swing of his scythe they mun fo'—
If yo'n root amung th' swathe, yo'n find doctors an' o."   *bundle*
     Derry Down.

Ill life—ill luck   EDWIN WAUGH

As I coom trailin' whoam fro th' town,
I co'de at th' sign o' th' Saddle,
To weet my whistle, an' keawer me down
For a crack wi' Jamie Raddle.   *chat*

Th' owd lad wur talkin' like a book,
Wi' some neighbour lads to mind him;   *listen to*
So I crept close by, i' th' chimbley nook,
Where I seldom fail to find him.

Said he: Yo known owd Bill at Kay's—
I never could abide him;
He's bin a wastrel o' his days,
An' wastrel luck betide him!
He's ta'en a job i' hond at last
That'll knock him into flinders,   *small pieces*
For they say'n he's boun' to buckle fast   *going*
Wi' buxom Mall o' Pinder's.

Mall's fresh an' strong, an' warm an' young,
An' frisky as a kitlin';   *kitten*
Billy's grey an' owd, an' worn an' cowd,
An' dwindled to a thwitlin'.   *shaving*
While th' fire o' life burns breet an' strong
I' bouncin' Mall o' Pinder's,
It's flickered down i' poor owd Bill
To nought but wanin' cinders.

He's done a deal o' careless wark,
An' never tried to mend it;
But he'll ha' to leave this cut i' th' dark   *piece of cloth*
For want o' leet to end it.
Both warp an' weft are rough an' strong,
An' off a mangy fleece, oh;
An' he'll be weary of his weighvin' long
Afore he downs his piece, oh.

He's shaked a free leg in his prime,
An' kicked at o' afore him;
He's flirted through his summertime,
Till winter's creepin' o'er him.
He's ta'en no kind mate to his breast
To make a lifelong friend on;
He's run his sands of life to waste,
And he's nought left to depend on.

Ill folk should tak ill fortin' well,
An' noather pout nor cry on 't;
For a mon that makes his bed his sel'
Should never grudge to lie on 't.
Then, lads, tak this last hint fro' me—
As through life's wood yo're wendin',
Don't run by every bonny tree,
An' tak to th' scrunt at th' endin'!   *brushwood*

J'

Good neet

JAMES DAWSON JUNIOR

Good neet, owd friend! aw wish thee well,
An' o thi family too;
May wisdom faithful in thee dwell,
Like folly in a foo'.

May o thi days be spent i' peace,
Like thoose o' which we sung
I' th' winter neets, at th' "Gowden Fleece,"
When thee an' me wur yung.

An' may thae never need to cringe
Before a titled Sur;
An honest workin' mon is th' hinge,
A lord is nobbut th' dur.

Be guided still, through weal or woe,
By thy dear spousie's tung;
For then, though foo's deny, aw know
Thae never con be wrung.

This world, thae knows, is full o'snares
To tangle honest men;
Thae rises, but ther's scores o' stairs
To help thee deawn ogen.

Just wipe thi specs, an' rub thi een,
An stretch thi up, owd mon!
Look where thae will, some vice is seen
Allurin' virtue on.

But no sich form eawr steps shall lure,
Though clothed i' garments smart;
We'll jog along wi' morals pure,
True noblemen i' heart.

Oft have we met, an' often still
As true friends may we meet;
Aw rank thee th' fost o' th' jovial crill—   *company*
Good neet, owd friend, good neet!

Thee an' me

SAMUEL LAYCOCK

Tha'rt livin' at thi country seat,
Amung o th' gents an' nobs;
Tha's sarvant girls to cook thi meat,

An' do thi bits o' jobs.
Aw'm lodgin' here wi' Bridget Yates,
At th' cot near th' Ceaw Lone Well;
Aw mend mi stockins, peel th' potates,
An' wesh mi shirts misel'!

Tha wears a finer cooat nor me;
Thi purse is better lined,
An' fortin's lavished moor o' thee,
Than th' rest o' human kind.
Life's storms 'at rage abeawt this yead,
An' pelt so hard at me—
'At mony a time aw've wished aw're dead,—   *so that*
But seldom trouble thee.

Tha'rt rich i'ole this world can give;
Tha's silver, an' tha's gowd;
But me—aw find it hard to live,
Aw'm poor, an' getten owd.
These fields an' lones aw'm ramblin' throo,
They o belung to thee;
Aw've nobbut just a yard or two
To ceawer in when aw dee.

When tha rides eawt th' folks o areawnd
Stond gapin' up at thee,
Becose tha'rt worth ten theawsand peawnd,
But scarcely notice me.
Aw trudge abeawt fro' spot to spot,
An' nob'dy seems to care:
They never seek my humble cot,
To ax me heaw aw fare.

If tha should dee, there's lots o' folk
Would fret an' cry, noa deawt:
When aw shut up, they'll only joke,
An' say, "He's just gone eawt!
Well, never heed him, let him goo,
An' find another port;
We're never to a chap or two,
We'n plenty moor o' th' sort."

Tha'll have a stone placed o'er thi grave
To show thi name an' age;
An' o tha's done 'at's good an' brave
Be seen i' history's page.
When aw get tumbled into th' greawnd,

Ther'll ne'er be nowt to show
Who's restin' 'neath that grassy meawnd,
An' nob'dy 'll want to know.

But deawn i' th' grave, what spoils o th' sport,
No ray o' leet con shoine;
An' th' worms 'll have hard wark to sort
Thy pampered clay fro' mine.
So, when this world for th' next tha swaps,
Tak' wi' thee under th' stone
Thi cooat ov arms, an' bits o' traps,   *finery*
Or else tha'll ne'er be known.

Pack up thi albert, hoop, an' pin,
An' opera-glass an' o;
Be sure tha sees 'em o put in,
Before tha gangs below.
Then iv some hungry worm should come
To root abeawt thi bones,
Tha may stond a better chance nor some
Iv its known tha'rt Mr Jones.

But up above, ther's One 'at sees
Thro' th' heart o' every mon;
An' He'll just find thi as tha dees,
So dee as weel as t' con.
An' when deawn here this campin' ends,
An' o eawr fau'ts forgiven,
Let thee an' me still show we're friends,
Bi shakin' honds i' heaven!

Owd Fogey   SAMUEL LAYCOCK

Owd Fogey lives i' Turner's Fowd,
Near Matty Wilson's schoo';
An' everybody knows him theer,
Becose he's sich a foo'.
Th' last week he pawned his Sunday clooas,
An' welly gan his tit,   *almost gave his*
An' neaw he hasn't a haupney left—   *horse away*
He's drunk it every bit.

He took their Jonny's Testament
To Barney Logan's sale,
An' th' bit o' brass he geet for that

He spent o' gin an' ale.
He's made away wi' lots o' things,
He's drunk his pig an' cote;
An' th' hens, an' th' ducks, an' th' pigeons, too,
They're o gone deawn his throat.

There's nowt ov ony value left,
Except poor Jane, his woife;
An' hoo's soa knocked abeawt i' th' world,
Hoo's weary ov her loife.
A week or two afore they'r wed
He took her on his knee,
An' swore he'd allus treat her weel,
But has he done? Not he.

His garden's covered o'er wi' weed,
An' th' fence is brocken deawn;
He used to have as noice a bit
As ony chap i' th' teawn.
He gan boath time an' labber then,   *labour*
He're in it every neet;
But neaw yo'd hardly give a groat
For o he has i' th' seet.   *in sight*

Th' last year he'd lots o' collyfleawers,
An' beons, an' peas, an' o;
He'd twenty furst-rate gooseberry trees,
An' sallary sticks to show.
He built a heawse for grooin' plants,
An' spent a peawnd o' glass,
But this he sowd to Farmer Jones,
An' had a spree wi' th' brass.

A pig he had worth thirty bob,
He sowd for seven an' six
To someb'dy deawn i' Kinder Lone—
It's just loike o his tricks.
He's reckless what he says or does,
For when he's soaked his clay
He cares for nowt nor nobody,
He'll give his things away.

Abeawt a month sin', Dan o' Bob's
Sowd off his poultry stock;
Owd Fogey went an' bowt 'em o—
He'd twenty an' a cock.
Th' next day he went to th' "Gapin' Goose,"

At th' bottom eend o' th' teawn,
An' sowd 'em o to Boniface,
For just a hawve a creawn.

He ceawered at th' aleheawse drinkin' grog,
Till twelve o'clock at neet;
An' when he reached his whoam th' next day,
He look'd a bonny seet.
His cooat wur daubed fro' top to tail
Wi' slurrin' deawn a broo;   *sliding   hill*
But nob'dy seemed to care a fig,
Becose he's sich a foo'.

Tha's noan so fur
to tramp, owd friend

SAMUEL LAYCOCK

Tha's noan so fur to tramp, owd friend;
Tha's welly reach'd thi journey's end;   *almost*
Trudge along.
Thi fiddle's mony a toime bin strung,
An' aw've no deawt bo what tha's sung
Mony a song.
But neaw, owd mon, thi days are few,
So, iv there's owt tha has to do,
Do it soon;
An' th' bit o' toime tha has to stop,
Get ready for another shop   *place*
Up aboon.   *above*

My piece is o bu'
woven eawt

RICHARD ROME BEALEY

My "piece" is o' bu' woven eawt,   *almost finished*
My wark is welly done:
Aw've "treddled" at it day by day,
Sin' th' toime 'ut aw begun.
Aw've sat i' th' loom-heawse long enough,
An' made th' owd shuttle fly;
An' neaw aw'm fain to stop it off,
An' lay my weyvin' by.

124

Aw dunnot know heaw th' piece is done;
Aw'm fear'd it's marr'd enough;   *afraid its spoiled*
Bu' th' warp wern't made o' th' best o' yarn,
An' th' weft were nobbut rough.
Aw've been some bother'd neaw an' then
Wi' knots, an' breakin's too;
They'n hamper'd me so mich at toimes
Aw've scarce known what to do.

Bu' th' Mester's just, an' weel He knows
'Ut th' yarn were none so good;
He winna "bate" me when He sees   *reduce my wages*
Aw've done as weel 's aw could.
Aw'se get my wage—aw'm sure o' that;
He'll gi'e me o 'ut's due,
An', mebbe, in His t'other place,
Some better wark to do.

Bu' then, aw reckon, 'tisn't th' stuff
We'n getten t' put i' th' loom,
Bu' what we mak' on't, good or bad,
'Ut th' credit on't 'll come.
Soem wark i' silk, an' other some
Ha'e cotton i' their gear;
Bu' silk or cotton matters nowt,
If nobbut th' skill be theere.

Bu' now it's nee' to th' eend o' th' week,
An' close to th' reckonin' day:
Aw'll tak my "piece" upon my back,
An' yer what th' Mester 'll say:
An' if aw nobbut yer His voice
Pronounce my wark "weel done,"
Aw'll straight forget o th' trouble past
I' th' pleasure 'ut's begun.

Tim Bobbin's grave   SAMUEL BAMFORD

I stood beside Tim Bobbin's grave
'At looks o'er Ratchda' teawn,   *Rochdale*
An' th' owd lad woke within his yerth,   *earth*
An' sed wheer arto' beawn.   *going*

"Om gooin' into th' Packer street,
As far as th' Gowden Bell,
To taste o' Daniel Kesmus ale."
Tim—I cud like a saup mysel'.

                                        sup (drink)

"An' by this hont o' my reet arm.
If fro' that hole theaw'll reawk,   *you'll get together*
Theaws't have a saup o' th' best breawn ale
'At ever lips did seawk."   *seek*

The greawnd it sturr'd beneath my feet,
An' then I yerd a groan;
He shook the dust fro' off his skull,
An' rowlt away the stone.

I brought him op o' a deep breawn jug,
'At a gallon did contain,
An' he took it at one blessed draught,
An' laid him deawn again.

Notes on the poems

People

Jone o' Grinfilt

Lancashire dialect poetry, as the poetry of a community, has always been strongly interested in people—their idiosyncracies, their problems and how they live together. This interest is clearly shown in one of the earliest and most famous poems in the dialect, "Jone o' Grinfilt." This is a song of which, according to Harland (*Ballads and Songs of Lancashire*) "more copies were sold among the rural population of Lancashire than of any other song known". It certainly stands as the precursor, and often the model, of nineteenth-century dialect poetry in Lancashire.

The story of its composition has been a matter of argument. Samuel Bamford (*Walks in South Lancashire*), whose story is repeated by Harland, tells of meeting "a little old-fashioned fellow with a wooden leg" in Ashton under Lyne called Joseph Coupe who claimed to have composed it, along with a man called Joseph Lees, while on a drinking spree and walking between Manchester and Oldham.

This account has been hotly disputed, and it seems more likely that Joseph Lees of Glodwick was the sole author (*cf. City News and Queries*, vol. 2, 1879, p. 130 and the *Ashton Reporter*, 14 June 1879), though Higson (*Jone o' Grinfilt and the Oldham Rushbearing*) acknowledges Coupe's part in making the ballad so popular.

The date of the poem is also difficult to fix exactly. The *Ashton Reporter* (1879) suggests that it was first performed at a Christmas supper given by Mr Beckett of Beckett Fold, Glodwick, "in the early part of the present century." Higson comments that the line concerning fighting "Oather

French, Dutch or Spanish" helps to fix such a date. Bateson (*History of Oldham*) relates that when England was threatened by invasion in 1803–04 Oldham raised three companies of Volunteers commanded by John Lees of Werneth, lord of the manor, which would tend to confirm a date somewhere around that time.

One of the more peculiar distinctions which this song earned was a performance before George III by the Lees Musical Society! The version given here is that printed in Harland's *Ballads and Songs of Lancashire*.

Th' Owdham weyver

Here is another poem in the "Jone o' Grinfilt" mould (indeed, it is often confusingly called "Jone o' Grinfilt" in its many broadside publications), but its social message is much stronger. It is a powerful reminder of the sufferings of the hand-loom weavers in the first half of the nineteenth century, before the power loom won its inevitable victory.

Like its namesake, the poem proved very popular, not least perhaps because of its subversive sentiments and its bitterness. A version of it was actually published by Elizabeth Gaskell in her novel *Mary Barton* (1848), where it is sung by Margaret Jennings, the working girl who goes blind but becomes locally famous as a singer. Mrs Gaskell says, "To read it, it may, perhaps seem humorous but it is that humour which is near akin to pathos, and to those who have seen the distress it describes it is a powerfully pathetic song."

It is noticeable, however, that though *Mary Barton* was regarded as a daringly radical novel Mrs Gaskell's version of the poem is toned down considerably. Verses 6, 8 and 9 as printed here are missing altogether and significant differences are noticeable elsewhere.

According to Harland, who is quoting his friend C. E. Higson, the poem was "taken down from the singing of an old hand-loom weaver at Droylsden". It was written just after the battle of Waterloo "when times were bad." (*Ballads and Songs of Lancashire*, p. 223).

The tune for the poem can be found in *Folk Song in England*, by A. L. Lloyd, and it can be heard on the record *Best o' t' Bunch* (Topic 12 TS 237). The version printed here is taken from a broadsheet in Harland's collection of ballads. It is obviously inconsistent in its rendering of dialect pronunciation, but I have not attempted to standardise it.

Verse 3. Mrs Gaskell has "tow'rt" for tarried. "Tow'rt" has the meaning of "just existed," which makes better sense here.

"Waterloo porridge" is presumably porridge made with water.

Verse 9. A reference to the navvying of the canal and railway age.

Th' mon at Mester Grundy's

This song, according to Sam Hill of Stalybridge (*Old Lancashire Songs and their Singers*, 1906), was first published at Ulverston in *Ashburner's New Vocal and Poetic Repertory* in 1807. It seems to me a very fine one, especially in its controlled, ironic comment upon the social climber. In the last verse, especially, the ironical significance of the final two lines, and the significance given to the word "content", seem quite remarkable for what Hill (and, following him, G. H. Whittaker in *A Lancashire Garland*, 1936) was satisfied to call "quaint dialect verse."

W. E. A. Axon records the poem in his *Folk Song and Folk Speech of Lancashire* (1870) and remarks that "it was at one time very popular in Lancashire, and gave rise to a phrase which is still occasionally heard, 'A mon o' Measter Grundy'."

Hill in 1906 was apparently unaware of Axon's book, for he tells of discovering the manuscript among some faded MSS, and comments again on the poem as a source "from whence comes the familiar household phrase, so much used in this locality".

It must certainly have been, as Axon suggests, a popular poem, as several broadside printings still survive. Indeed, the version given here is from a Harkness broadside (Harris Library, Preston) which seems slightly superior poetically to the versions of either Axon or Hill.

Friends are few when folks are poor

I have not found this poem recorded in any dialect anthology, but it seems yet again a powerful cry against the social injustices of the first half of the nineteenth century. It is, indeed, a neat reversal of the "Mon at Mester Grundy's" situation.

Probably it was written between 1835 and 1850, as there is a reference in verse 5 to the overseers and guardians of the new poor law (1834), and the poem with which it is printed on a broadside has a reference to the Mormons, who were also a phenomenon of the 1830s.

Several copies of this broadside, which has no printer's name on it, are to be found in the Harris Library at Preston.

Eawr folk

This is the first poem in the anthology by Edwin Waugh, arguably the greatest of the dialect poets, and it clearly reveals that warm-hearted tolerance and joy in his fellow men which is so much a feature of his poetry.

Poems cataloguing relations, friends and neighbours have been very common in Lancashire dialect writing since the middle of the nineteenth century. In this anthology are included Laycock's "Bowton's Yard" and Fitton's "Cotton Fowd," but one might also remember John Trafford Clegg's "Twenty Row," and, in modern times, Harvey Kershaw's "Best o' t' bunch," both within the same tradition.

An interesting echo of this kind of poetry can also be found in Ted Hughes of Heptonstall's *Meet my Folks* (1961).

"Eawr folk" first appeared in book form in the 1870 edition of Waugh's poems. Throughout the anthology the version of the poems by Waugh which is given is that of the *Collected Works*.

Tum Rindle

In a poem like this, celebrating the conviviality of simple living, Edwin Waugh is, I think, at his best. There is a warm humanity in his writing which makes this catalogue of people far more than a mere catalogue. In another poem, "Forgive one another," which is not included in this anthology because of its rather over-moralising tone, Waugh quotes a Lancashire saying which seems to sum up his own attitude to humanity: "We're o' Johnny Butteroth's lads"—in other words, "we're all brothers." This tolerance and broad humanity are to be found in much of his poetry and are certainly reflected here. "Tum Rindle" first appeared in book form in the 1870 edition of Waugh's poems.

Verse 4. "Moston Sam" must refer to Waugh's friend Samuel Bamford, who lived in Moston in his later years.

The little doffer

A doffer is someone who takes away the full bobbins or spindles in a mill. The overlooker is, of course, the equivalent of a foreman. A simple story but skilfully told. A sung version of this poem will be found on Topic record 12 T 188, *Deep Lancashire*. It is one of Waugh's later poems, appearing first in the collected edition of his work.

The weaver of Wellbrook

This is the only poem in the anthology by Ben Brierley, which may seem short measure for a writer who was equalled only by Waugh in the national reputation he built up as a dialect writer. However, most people would admit that his most effective writing was in prose, and his poetry, though often very competent, is not the base on which his reputation rests.

This poem in fact is part of a story called *The Chronicles of Waverlow*, published in 1863. Ben Brierley himself appeared in dramatised versions of the story and sang the weaver's song—an interesting reminder that as a young man he had himself been a hand-loom weaver in Bolton just before the final triumph of the power-loom. This, no doubt, accounts for the confidence with which Brierley has incorporated the technical language

130

of weaving into his poem. But what is even more remarkable is the success with which he seems to have captured the movement of the loom in the movement of the verse.

Chorus:

Linderins: ropes put round the beam when the fabric is nearly finished. Yealdhook: hook for the wires which keep the warp threads separated.

Bowton's Yard

This is the first poem by Samuel Laycock to appear in the anthology. It is typical of Laycock at his best, witty yet very warm-hearted. In his praise of "Yawshur folk" it might be remembered that Laycock himself came from Yorkshire, and his comment that he is "th' only chap as doesn't drink" is also a reminder that Laycock was a very eloquent teetotaller.

Later Laycock produced two poems, "Quality Row" and "A second visit to Quality Row," which are rather similar to "Bowton's Yard," though they deal with a rather more high-class group of people. They are not, I think, half as good, half as human, as this early poem.

According to G. H. Whittaker (*Some Stalybridge Songs and their Singer*, 1944), Bolton's Yard was still standing in 1933.

A sung version of the poem will be found on Topic record 12 T 104, *Owdham Edge*.

Except where specified, the versions of Laycock's poems in this anthology are those of the *Collected Writings* edition.

Mi grondfeyther

This is a description of events in Laycock's boyhood at his grandfather's house at Intake Head, near Marsden. I think it conveys a real sense of the adventures of boyhood and affection for the old man whilst just about avoiding sentimentality. Printed here is an early version of the poem, much more effective than the limp version of the *Collected Writings*.

Verse 2. Th' Owd Book is, of course, the Bible.

Cotton Fowd

Finally in this section a poem by Sam Fitton to remind us of the strength of tradition in Lancashire dialect verse. Not only does this poem look back to "Eawr folk" and "Bowton's Yard" in subject matter, it also copies them technically in metre. This poem, nevertheless, I think, lacks the variety and humanity of Waugh and Laycock, and although it has something of the wit which informs most of Fitton's work it is a good example of the way in which later dialect poetry has become more artificial and less grounded in experience.

Fairs and festivities

Warikin Fair

Significant centres of communal activity are, of course, the varied festivities which have traditionally lightened humdrum and difficult lives. Lancashire dialect poetry is rich in descriptions of such festivities (though, significantly, there are fewer in the later nineteenth century than earlier), and, somewhat indirectly, what is generally regarded as the earliest dialect poem, "Warikin Fair," is about such a subject. The poem must have been composed in the mid-sixteenth century, since Raunley Shay (Randle Shaw) was a bailiff for Sir Thomas Butler in 1548.

As the "original" Lancashire dialect poem, "Warikin Fair" has been much anthologised. The most commonly quoted version is that offered by John Harland in *Ballads and Songs of Lancashire*. Here, however, I have taken J. O. Halliwell's version from his *Dictionary of Archaic and Provincial Words*, vol. I. This seems to me more natural and lively, particularly in its ending.

Warikin is, of course, the modern Warrington.

A sung version of this poem will be found on Topic record 12 TS 236, *A Lancashire Man*.

Droylsden Wakes song

The first two poems in this section both describe conflict between married people, and both describe the woman more than holding her own. The traditional theme of the henpecked husband remains very popular in dialect poetry right up to the present day.

The Wakes song was a feature of Droylsden festivities in the early years of the nineteenth century. Harland (*Ballads and Songs of Lancashire*) says that it was actually sung by two men, one dressed as a woman, and both riding horses. They pretended to spin flax with the old-style spinning wheels, and collected money from the crowd.

A sung version of this poem can be found on Topic record 12 T 104, *Steam Whistle Ballads*. The version offered here is that printed in Harlands *Ballads and Songs of Lancashire*.

Jone's ramble fro' Owdam to Karsy Moor races

This lively song was also a great favourite in the earlier part of the nineteenth century. It is quoted extensively in Harland's essays "Songs of the working classes" in the *Manchester Guardian* of December 1839. It is the first poem in this anthology by one of the Wilsons, whose work received considerable publicity from that date onwards.

The poem celebrates the Manchester races and fair held for many years on Kersall Moor, three miles north of the city. The last race meeting there was held during Whit week, 1846—afterwards the event was moved to the Castle Irwell grounds. Its title plainly acknowledges the influence of "Jone o' Grinfilt," as do a host of dialect poems written in the first half of the century.

In the last verse "eawr six-bell" refers to the six o'clock bell at the factory—an early hint of the new industrial life. But many of the references in the early part of the poem are to traditional pastimes, many of which have now been forgotten.

Johnny Green's description of Tinker's Gardens

This poem, by the youngest of the Wilsons, seems also to have been extremely popular. In his 1842 edition of the Wilson poems Alexander Wilson recounts that he "wrote it in my father's shop some fifteen years ago" and that it was publicised by the actor, Mr Gates. Though there is no reason to doubt Wilson's account, the reference to "God save eawr noble Queen" in v. 11, followed in the next verse by a reference to the King's "creawnation", suggests that, as with most rhymes first composed for recitation, additions were made to the poem later on. This poem is also mentioned in Harland's "Songs of the working classes," and it was then anthologised (along with "Karsy Moor") in Elijah Riding's *The Lancashire Muse* (1853). In *Sketches of Lancashire Life* (1855) Edwin Waugh, walking to the cottage of Tim Bobbin at Milnrow, describes some weavers, during a break from work, "humming one of Alexander Wilson's songs"—"Tinker's Gardens."

The gardens themselves were a popular place for Manchester people to enjoy themselves at weekends from the late eighteenth century onwards. Started by a man called Tinker, they were situated just by the Rochdale road, and from 1814 onwards officially (but not by the patrons) were called Vauxhall Gardens. They closed down in 1852. (*Cf.* T. Swindells, *Manchester Streets and Manchester Men*, fifth series.)

Jack, goo peawn thi fiddle

This little verse is recorded in *City News, Notes and Queries*, vol. 5 (1883–84), where Mrs Linnaeus Banks recalls hearing it "more than fifty years ago".

Going to the fair

This is one of Edwin Waugh's later poems and plainly lacks the vivacity or the detailed descriptions of the Wilson poems, or indeed of Waugh's own earlier poetry. It is interesting, however, in revealing the peculiar ambivalence with which Waugh seems to have regarded communal merrymaking outside the home, as compared with merrymaking within the home. As in "Come whoam to thi childer" (p. 64), he seems to be fascinated by the attractiveness of fairs while taking a very puritan position concerning their wickedness. The dialogue form, a device he frequently uses, enables him to have his cake and eat it too in this respect.

The City Fathers seem to have shared Waugh's misgivings about the fair. It was a popular Easter occasion which had been held since the opening of the Bridgewater Canal, but it was abolished, because of the unseemly goings on, in 1876 (*cf.* L. M. Hayes, *Reminiscences of Manchester*, and *Proceedings* of the Manchester Literay Club).

The poem first appeared in the collected edition of Waugh's works.

Rachda Wakes

Festivities at the end of the nineteenth century are here represented in two poems by John Trafford Clegg, "Rachda Wakes" and "Th' Infirmary day." Both were written round about 1890. It is interesting to note the changes that have come over fairs during the century and how much more recognisable the activities are. At the same time, of course, the dialect poetry has become more sophisticated, and to that extent, I believe, less immediate and direct.

Th' Infirmary day

Despite the moralising ending to this poem I have included it here partly because of its lively description of the festivities at the beginning and partly because of the contrast which comes across so clearly between the short pleasures of a holiday and the long dangers of a working life. It is also a reminder of the way in which social services such as hospitals had begun to grow up during the century to meet the needs of a massive group of working people. There was no purpose-built hospital in Rochdale until 1883. Between 1887 and 1896 annual galas were held to provide money for extensions.

Eawr market neet

A typical example of Sam Fitton's humorous and observant writing, this poem reminds us of the gaiety and liveliness of the old-style town markets and the many eccentric characters to be found there.

A sung version can be found on Topic record 12 TS 206, *Oldham's Burning Sands*.

Owdham footbo'

A short, simple poem by a relatively recent dialect poet, just as a reminder of the changes in entertainment which the growth in the popularity of football, both soccer and Rugby League, brought to working people in Lancashire at the turn of the century.

Love

The country wedding

The tradition of love poetry in the Lancashire dialect is rather a mixed one. There are some very effective poems in the early and mid-nineteenth century, particularly by Edwin Waugh, but many later ones are sickeningly sentimental. Later poems concerning love, if they are effective at all, are effective because they make fun of it. In this context "The country wedding" by Thomas Wilson, despite its clumsiness, has merits which are often lacking in later love poems.

It is certainly free of the coyness which later infected the poetry. So much so, in fact, that Harland, editing this poem in 1865, missed out at least one verse following v. 7 as printed here. Since the poem had not been published in earlier editions of *The Songs of the Wilsons*, and had presumably been given him by one of the two remaining Wilson brothers, William, I have been unable to trace an uncensored version. In the 1865 edition Harland remarks that the poem was written when Thomas Wilson was nineteen, which would probably date it about 1800–10.

"Scowlin Joshua" in v. 6 is the Rev. Joshua Brookes, eccentric, chaplain of the Manchester parish church from 1791 to 1821, and traditional enemy of the Wilsons. W. E. A. Axon remarks (*Bygone Lancashire*, ed. E. Axon) that "Brookes was said to have married more people than any other clergyman in the kingdom."

The Lancashire witch

W. E. A. Axon (*Folk Song and Folk Speech of Lancashire*) remarks that this is "one of the most perfect lyrics in the Lancashire dialect, if not, indeed, the best of its love poems." It is especially effective because of the skilful way in which the natural dialect is married to the song-like verse. It is also an early example of a tradition in dialect writing which Waugh strengthened—love seen from the point of view of the woman, not the man.

The title, of course, refers to the famous witches of Pendle who were hanged at Lancaster in the sixteenth century.

The dule's i' this bonnet o' mine

This is the first of three love poems in the anthology by Edwin Waugh. There are several interesting points to make about it. In the first place

K

this, like many other of Waugh's poems, was intended to be sung—there is a lyrical quality about his poetry which reflects this. Secondly Waugh confirmed traditions in dialect love poetry which were copied, sometimes slavishly, by later writers. Here he takes up the theme of love from the woman's point of view, as Scholes had done, and as many less gifted later poets were to do. Although, in the middle of the nineteenth century, he is much less open about sexual passion than the Wilsons had been earlier, it is plain that these Lancashire girls are not the passionless females of some better known nineteenth-century literature.

This and the two love poems which follow were first published in 1858, and are therefore among Waugh's earliest dialect poems.

What ails thee, my son, Robin?

Here Waugh plainly adopts the familiar oral tradition of the ballads in presenting a discussion about the pains of love in the form of a dialogue between mother and son. And plainly, again, the poem is intended for singing.

Come, Mary, link thi arm i' mine

Part of the interest of this poem lies in the description of the simple things which made up the household for newly married people when Waugh was writing. Cataloguing household possessions is an almost obsessive interest of dialect writers in the nineteenth century, and no doubt relates to the extreme insecurity of the time—with the threat of unemployment, and the bailiffs on the doorsteps, as instanced in several poems in this anthology.

It is also interesting to note that, particularly in his love poetry, Waugh is looking backwards to an earlier, rural and less complicated life. Whereas poetry on other themes seems contemporary and is generally based on industrial and town life, love poetry still tends to talk about the country and the cottage.

The ending of v. 1 in this poem seems to have given Waugh some trouble. Early versions of the poem have for l. 6 "a bonny *gem* of wet." In the 1859 edition of his poems after l. 4 the poem continues:

> There's a little cot beside yon spring
> An' iv thae'll share't wi' me
> Aw'll buy tho th' prattist gowden ring
> That ever theaw did see.

And then straight on to v. 3 of the version given here.

136

Coaxin'

This is the first poem in the anthology by Joseph Ramsbottom, better known for his poetry of the Cotton Famine than for his love poetry. It first appeared in *Country Words*, a short-lived journal of Lancashire culture which was published in 1866 and 1867.

The poem seems to me a fair example of Ramsbottom's strengths and weaknesses. It is sentimental and, compared with Waugh's poetry, technically rough. At the same time there is a particular concreteness about his images, and a rightness about some of his phrasing—"Eawt o' th' days we wortch to live, We may tak' one day to love," for example— which makes Ramsbottom one of the most effective Lancashire poets.

Stop wi' thi mother

Nearly all Ramsbottom's writing is to be found during the 1860s, but this is an unusually late poem, appearing in the Manchester Literary Club *Papers* in 1884. It is interesting to note that it is written in the same metre as "Jone o' Grinfilt."

It also raises some interesting questions. Is Ramsbottom making a plea for thriftiness before marriage, along conventional self-help lines? Or is he making fun of the sillinesses of young love, as later dialect writers were increasingly to do? Or is he simply satirising a possessive mother?

Perhaps something of all three. Ramsbottom's particular gifts as a poet are still evident here, despite the unlikely title. Not many poets would reach the uncomfortable realism in describing poverty and distress that marks v. 5.

Neaw aw'm a married mon

This is a most unusual poem in dialect writing terms because of its intense personal feeling. It is unusual, too, in deliberately repudiating the idea that marriage should wait till it can be afforded, and in suggesting that woman's work might also be a man's work as well. This poem, and "There's nowt loike spinnin' shoddy' (p. 89), show Burgess as a much more radical figure than most of his contemporaries.

There is a very sad story attached to it. Written in 1875, the poem was published "in memoriam," for within one month of this eagerly awaited marriage his wife was dead from tubercolosis.

Yon weyver as warks t' beeam to me

Compared with the previous poem, this seems empty of genuine feeling, despite its greater technical accomplishment. It is interesting, however, as illustrating the increasingly moralising tone which crept into love poetry at the end of the century, with a condemnation of flirtatiousness that seems a long way removed from "The Lancashire witch".

Verse 1. piecin' mi bad sides and mashes: putting right flaws in the cloth.

Eawr Sarah's getten a chap
Eawr Joe

The two poems which complete this section (the one plainly heavily influenced by the other) illustrate the most commonly successful type of love poetry written by dialect writers in the twentieth century.

Both, very wittily, make fun of the foolishness of love, and in particular satirise the social pretensions which love can encourage. In this perhaps they give unconscious evidence to the breaking up of the closely knit society amongst whom dialect writing could flourish.

A sung version of "Eawr Sarah's getten a chap" will be found on Topic record 12 T 204, *Owdham Edge*.

"*Eawr Joe,*" *v. 1.* A piecer joins up the threads in the spinning process. The jinny gate is the passage between the spinning jennies (*cf.* also "Hard times" (p. 95) by Whitehead).

Home

Edwin Waugh.is pre-eminently the poet of the home, and so in this section five of his poems are represented. Yet for most of the dialect writers the values of home life were very important, and they actively promoted them in a way which may seem rather sentimental to us but which may have seemed much less so in days of poverty, homelessness and prospects of early death.

An old toast

This is quoted by Waugh in his book *The Chimney Corner* (*Collected Works*, vol. 8, p. 293).

Come whoam to thi childer an' me

This was the poem that made Edwin Waugh famous. First published in 1856 in the *Manchester Examiner*, it established his reputation as one of the finest dialect poets when it appeared in pamphlet form. Lady Burdett-Coutts, the reformer and friend of Dickens, was much impressed by it and actively promoted its sale, not only in England but abroad as well. Many poets, including Laycock, refer to it in their own work, and it was widely imitated. In a very real sense this poem, with all its faults, put Lancashire dialect poetry on the map.

Indeed, in many ways it is typical of dialect poetry in the second half of the nineteenth century. It is domestic and it supports domestic values, particularly faithfulness between man and wife. It is down-to-earth in its descriptions of simple home life. At the same time it could certainly be accused of sentimentality. Many of Waugh's friends and contemporaries recognised this, and some of the imitations are in fact parodies. Ben Brierley, for instance, wrote one called "Go tak thi ragg'd childer an' flit" (i.e. move house) and William Billington wrote one called "A tay and rum ditty."

Though the poem looks forward to later dialect poetry in both its strengths and weaknesses, it is interesting to note that it also looks back to "Warikin Fair" and the Droylsden Wakes song in using the form of a dispute between man and wife as a dramatic situation.

The tune for "Come whoam" can be found in John Graham's *Dialect Songs of the North*, where Graham remarks that it was "hummed all over Lancashire". Another reminder that Waugh's poetry was intended for singing.

Neet-fo

"Nightfall." Edwin Waugh's ideal! An industrious woman, a working husband, a spick-and-span home, a new baby, real affection between man and wife, and a meal to come home to. An ideal, too, which is commonly presented, though not often so fluently, by other dialect poets. The home indeed stood for security in a very insecure world. Note how Waugh stresses the joy of what might seem a very ordinary occasion, the wife "hutching" with glee and even the water-drops from the tap seeming alive. It is interesting also to see Waugh, as in so many of his poems, writing from the woman's point of view, and stressing the affection between man and woman from the woman's, not the man's, side.

The poem appeared in the 1870 edition of his poetry.

Margit's comin

The reverse side of the coin—a shrewish wife and a feckless husband. The moral surely lies in v. 4:

> If folk were nobbut o' i' th' mind
> To make their bits o' booses kind,
> There'd be less wanderin' eawt to find
> A corner to be quiet in.

But Waugh's humorous and dramatic presentation of the situation is much more acceptable than some of the sermons which are preached in dialect verse, for instance by Laycock, about being good wives and husbands.

The reference to Garibaldi and the fall of kings recalls the campaign for the unification of Italy in the 1850s. Garibaldi set up a farm on the island of Caprera, hence the joke about selling milk (v. 6).

This is an early poem: it appeared in the 1861 edition of Waugh's poetry.

Dinner time

The moral as before. Here perhaps more evidently in this later poem Waugh shows an insensitivity to the wife's point of view—a person who has "nought to do, fro' morn to neet, but keep things clean an' straight"—which is often echoed by other dialect writers. The wife's job is certainly seen as ministering to a tired husband at the expense of her own social life.

The dramatic presentation, with two characters speaking, obviously for performance, is in a long tradition of dialect writing in both prose and verse. The poem was published in the collected edition of Waugh's work.

Down again!

It is rather surprising, perhaps, to see childbirth as the subject of a nineteenth-century poem—even a humorous poem. But Waugh handles the subject well, with real human feeling breaking through effectively in the last two verses.

Verse 8. Red-shank: "applied figuratively and contemptuously to any bare or red-legged person. It has been commonly used in Lancashire ever since the retreat of the bare-legged Scotch rebels in 1745." (*A Glossary of the Lancashire Dialect*, Part 2, ed. Nodal and Milner). The poem was published in the collected edition of Waugh's work.

Eawr Jack

A poem of the mid 1860s, very much in the Waugh mould but without his lively power. It is, however, I believe, easily the best of Mellor's poems.

Welcome, bonny brid!

Laycock composed this fine poem while his child was actually being born. He sat down in a corner of the room and wrote it then and there. It was a period of great distress because of the Cotton Famine (*cf.* Section 6), and one can imagine his mingled joy and anxiety. Laycock himself said that he felt he had written the poem under a kind of inspiration.

As a matter of fact, although the poem is addressed to a son the baby turned out to be a daughter! She was always a great favourite, and Laycock wrote several poems about her, including one for her wedding. "Bonny brid" became a great favourite in Lancashire and is perhaps the best known of dialect poems. Many other poets refer to it, and it has been included in many anthologies.

The image of the home as a nest and the family as birds is a common one with Laycock and with other dialect poets (*cf.*, for instance, "Come, Mary, link thi arm i' mine," v. 8). It suggests how important the home was as a place of comfort and security to people working long hours in poor and uncertain conditions. Even after a hundred years the poem seems to capture in a very moving way the inevitable conflict between natural affection for a newborn baby and the practical hardships of life. It was published first as one of the twelve lyrics of the Cotton Panic which made Laycock famous (*cf.* Section 6).

A sung version will be found on Topic record 12 TS 215, *Transpennine*.

Wimmen's wark es niver done

This poem betrays more sympathy, despite its moralising ending, for the woman's point of view than we find in Waugh's poetry of home life. It gives a real feeling of the drudgery of things.

Many dialect poems, when they were not intended to be sung, were written for recitation, as an advertisement for Laycock's poems has it, "at Band of Hope Meetings and Social Gatherings." This tradition has persisted into the present day, and it might be in "Darby and Joan" clubs or their equivalent that one would now be most likely to hear dialect poetry. Plainly this poem—and several others in this anthology—are intended for such an audience. It first appeared in a pamphlet, *Echoes from a Lancashire Vale*, published in 1873.

Th' childer's holiday

A typical Sam Fitton poem, and Fitton at his best, not labouring the jokes too much. A sung version will be found on Topic record 12 TS 206, *Oldham's Burning Sands*.

Work

Life in the mills, in the factories and in the pits has not often been the subject of conventional poetry. In Lancashire dialect poetry, on the other hand, manual work, or the lack of it, is one of the main themes. In the poems which follow, often written by the factory workers themselves, we can see something of the pleasures and pains of the ordinary worker.

Rambles in Owdham, and peep into the workshops

This vigorous song gives a unique picture of working life in Oldham during the 1850s. The version printed here is taken from *Gaskel's Comic Song Book*, a popular collection of the day, though it appeared also as a broadsheet.

The song rests firmly in the oral tradition of "Jone o' Grinfilt" and the songs of the Wilsons, particularly in in its catalogue of sights and its use of the ramble as the framework for the verse. But in making the factory the object of description it moves into the industrial age. "In Owdham streets at dinner time" (also in *Gaskel's Song Book*), where the verse is in standard English, and an inferior, much older but apparently more popular dialect poem, "Owd Ned's a rare strong chap", are other examples of this interesting development. A feature of the poem is the confidence and the optimism which the new discoveries were bringing to working people.

The "new" Market Hall (v. 3) in Oldham was opened in 1856 on the site of the old Tommyfield market.

"Neddy engine" (v. 6). "Ned" was a popular name for the steam engines in the factories. "Owd Ned's a rare strong chap" is about a steam engine.

Verses 9 and 15. This turn-out may refer to events in February 1857, when a short-time committee tried to prevent the masters evading the terms of the Factory Act of 1850. They were unsuccessful.

Verse 10. Temples keep the cloth stretched to its proper width during weaving. Cops hold the thread for the machines.

The factory worker's song

This fragment is recorded in *Some Lancashire Rhymes* by John Mortimer (Manchester Literary Club *Papers*, 1890). It probably refers to events in August 1842—the "great turn-out," which lasted for six weeks and resulted in some of the workers being transported. (*Cf.* S. Hill, *Bygone Stalybridge*). Not only a lively song but a very bitter one, its immediacy contrasts markedly with Mary Thomason's "Strike song" a century later.

The factory bell

The force of this poem rests in the last verse, where the factory workers' condition is compared with that of less regimented and overworked people. The poem was published in the collected edition of Waugh's work.

Hard weather

Waugh's songs about hard times are always slightly disappointing. They seem to accept the situation too easily, to sing about it too much—a sign perhaps that Waugh himself was never directly concerned in industrial life. Nevertheless this poem, written during one of the ever-recurring slumps in trade (though in v. 4 it almost forsakes the dialect altogether), does give a vivid idea of the hardship so common in Lancashire even in the later nineteenth century. It was published in the collected edition of Waugh's work.

There's nowt loike spinnin' shoddy

This is a difficult poem, both because it has a large number of technical words and because it attempts to imitate so faithfully the local dialect. But it is well worth making the effort to understand, since it is certainly the angriest poem in the whole anthology.

Burgess conveys in a most realistic way the hardships of work in the spinning mills and, as might be expected of one who was later to become a pioneer of the labour movement, he has a very clear view of the way in which people were exploited. The speaker is a young boy, still no more than ten, but having to get up at five o'clock every morning and work at spinning shoddy (cotton put together from the left-overs of the better cotton).

In his autobiography Burgess writes, "The poem . . . is a composite picture of my experiences as a piecer at Robin Ogden's, Sett; Besson's, Droylsden; and Boundary Mill, Mills Hill. The ill usage described was all experienced at Robin Ogden's, where I had an Irish minder named Dillon. He was the only man who ever laid a finger on me in the way of chastisement. I was then under ten years of age."

In the first four lines we see how the employers looked upon shoddy spinning—as a means to a quick profit in an age of "speculation", but from then onwards we see it from the "hands' " point of view—as a form of slavery.

Verse 1. A reference to the biblical story of the Israelites in Egypt as slaves having to make bricks without straw.

Verse 2. "Top-clearer laps an' rovin's, under-clearer waste an' fly." Raw cotton first lapped, then put through the roving frame ready for the carding process. It was the waste from these processes which came to the shoddy spinner.

"Scrutcht an' carded": after carding the cotton is thin enough to spin.

Verse 3. Idleback: scouring stone. Burgess implies that it is better to be a rag-and-bone man than to spin shoddy.

Verse 5. Refers to the practice of starting the engine (and hence the machines) early and stopping it late, in order to get more work from the spinners than was paid for.

Verse 6. Ends: broken threads.

A sung version of this poem will be found on Topic record 12 TS 236, *A Lancashire Man*.

A weighver's song

In contrast, this lively poem captures more fully than any other an aspect of work in the mills which is not so often emphasised—the enjoyment and the sense of mastery which it sometimes gave even to the operatives. It appeared in Clegg's *Reaund bi t' Derby* in 1890, along with "Rachda' Wakes" (p. 37).
A sung version will be found on Topic record 12 TS 215, *Transpennine*.

Hawf past five at neet
Six o' clock at mornin'

These two pieces, in the Blackburn dialect, are further reminders of the tyrrany of the factory bell in its demands upon working people.
Baron's verse is technically rather sophisticated for dialect writing, with intricate rhythms and rhyme schemes, but it does not get *within* its subject matter as well as, for instance, the simpler poetry of Burgess.

Strike song

Two twentieth-century poems to end this section. Mary Thomason's appeared in *Warp and Weft*, published in 1938, a year after her death. Despite the title of the book, the poem obviously concerns a pit strike, and the sympathy of the writer is plainly with the strikers.
A sung version will be found on the record *Deep Lancashire* (Topic 12 T 188).

Hard times

This section of the anthology began and ends at Oldham. The two poems are separated by a hundred years, but they suggest a continuance of industrial experience faithfully chronicled in dialect poetry. Whitehead's moving poem, indeed, in looking back over years of hardship, is a strong reminder of the resilience of ordinary people in persistently difficult times.
Verse 1. Head stocks: the part of the spinning mule which holds the mechanism.

The Cotton Panic

"A Bible-woman, engaged in her loving work in one of the most distressed localities in Lancashire, said to a poor little girl,—'My dear, do you know the meaning of sorrow?' 'Want of cotton,' replied the child." (A. F. Henslow, *Cotton and the want of it*, 1863).

Work in the cotton industry was never secure: the trade was always one of the first to feel the effects of the periodic booms and slumps of the Victorian economy. The prolonged decline of the hand-loom weaving industry was recognised as a source of hardship for people in Lancashire for several decades. Nevertheless the American civil war of 1861–64, with the blockade of trade by the northern states, which stopped cotton imports very effectively, was a time of even greater suffering than usual.

The workers' plight certainly caught the imagination of the country, and voluntary relief schemes were organised on a wide scale. It also caught the imagination of the dialect poets: a great number of street broadsides were produced for local consumption, although many poems were obviously aimed also at the wider audience of those who were organising relief, and appeal directly or indirectly for help.

The most remarkable productions of these years were Laycock's famine songs (twelve in number), which were published as broadsheets and in the Stalybridge press, and Ramsbottom's *Lancashire Rhymes*, published in book form in 1864.

Th' Surat weyver

This poem is in the Blackburn dialect and appeared first as a broadsheet in Blackburn during the Panic. According to W. W. Skeat (*Bibliographical list: Dialects*, 1873), 14,000 copies were sold in this form, largely during the Panic. It certainly has a vigour and attack which are often lacking even in the poetry of Laycock.

"Surat" (or "Shurat") is short staple cotton from the Surat area of India, which was obviously considered a poor substitute for the American cotton because it broke so easily.

Verse 3. The treadmill and picking oakum (as other poems in this section also record), along with breaking stones for road building, were the tasks people were commonly put to if they applied for relief or had to go to the workhouse.

It is interesting that, although it has commonly been believed that the Lancashire people showed an almost heroic devotion to the anti-slavery cause, considering that it was the Northerners (the "Yankees") who were depriving them of cotton, there are one or two signs in this and other poems that the Yankees were not altogether popular.

The source of this version is the broadsheet in Harland's manuscripts (1865) in the Manchester Central Library.

The Shurat weaver's song

In Stalybridge Laycock also wrote his song about "Shurat"—one of the twelve which were to make him locally famous. Many of them, says George Milner in his introduction to the second edition of Laycock's *Col-*

lected Writings (1908), were "Learnt by heart and sung by the lads and lasses" in the streets of Stalybridge" (*cf.* Introduction, p. 4).

Verse 2. "Cuts" refers to pieces of cloth when woven. "Dressed": a mixture of flour and water was put on the thread to stop it breaking too easily. Too much would defeat the purpose, but "Surat" obviously required too much.

Another song about Surat, of less merit, appeared in *Notes and Queries* for 3 June 1865. According to the writer, "T. N.," of Bacup, this song was a great favourite of the people of Dean, in Rossendale, who were famous as singers—"the Deyghn Layrocks (Larks)" (*cf.* Edwin Waugh "Wails of the workless poor," *Lancashire Sketches*, third edition, p. 276):

> I look at th' yealds, and there they stick,
> I ne'er seed th' like sin' I wur wick [alive.]
> What pity could befal a heart
> To think about these hard-sized warps.

Philip Clough's tale

The first of Ramsbottom's *Lancashire Rhymes: Phases of Distress* in this anthology. Ramsbottom captures better than anybody the dreariness of being out of work—though sometimes, perhaps, running the danger of making the poem itself dreary.

For "pooin' oakum" and "breakin' stones" see the note to "Th' Shurat weyver," above.

Th' owd pedlar

Again by Ramsbottom, this poem is a reminder that it was not only the operatives who suffered from the depression. There is a poem on a similar theme, "Th' owd barber eawt o' wark," among Laycock's famine songs.

Here, and in many of his poems, Ramsbottom puts an "h" after dental consonants to suggest the softening which occurs in dialect speech. If the "h" is ignored the meaning of several words which may appear unusual will become clear.

It's hard to ceawer i' th' chimney nook

Like Ramsbottom in "Philip Clough's tale," Laycock here catalogues the difficulties of making ends meet. The interest in both poems lies partly in the nature of those possessions which were available for sale.

Verse 3. For "th' Refuge sewin' class" see the notes on "Sewin' class song," below.

Frettin'

Perhaps the most doleful of all the Panic songs, this poem nevertheless contains some of Ramsbottom's most memorable lines—notably the last two, and, in v. 5, his vivid image of the workmen dependent upon charity: "poor propt up things ut conno stond."

Aw've turned me bit o' garden o'er

This simple poem provides some contrast to the pervading gloom of the preceding ones, and is perhaps a reminder that one of the characteristics of the mill workers during the Panic is said to have been their resilience.

Eawr factory skoo

This rough song is to be found in broadsheet form in Harland's collection of MSS. During the slump, as part of the charitable activities, schools were set up for the unemployed workers. If we judge from the dialect verse, they seem to have been successful, and for many provided the first opportunity to learn to read and write.

Verse 3. The "rule of three" was commonly taught in elementary schools for calculating proportions.

Sewin' class song

This is Laycock's poem on much the same theme. During the Panic, while schools were organised for the men, these "sewing classes" were provided for the women. Actually, with one eye on the people providing the money for the schools, Laycock is not at his best. There are here a prosiness and a moralising tone which often mar his later poetry. However, it is interesting to see how much these schools seem to have caught the imagination of at least some sections of the working class.

Verse 2. "Cutters out" would be the people who cut the cloth out, ready for it to be sewn.

Gooin' t' schoo'

Despite some sentimentality in the ending, Ramsbottom captures better than the others the mixed feelings of the working man given the chance of some kind of basic education in those unhappy times—hurt pride at relying on charity, some embarrassment at his own ignorance, and a quick understanding, nevertheless, of the benefits he has gained.

Aw wod this war wur ended

This heartfelt cry from Billington, dated 1863, echoes in realistic terms the feelings of many unemployed workers during the Panic. Billington's poetry of this time has a rude force which conveys clearly the sense of suffering and, above all, the waste of energy and ability brought about by unemployment.

Old age

Old age and death are a frequent topic of the dialect poets. Their treatment may at times seem sentimental, but many of the poems show an insight into the loneliness, the dignity—and, indeed, the comedy—of old age which is worthy of consideration.

Owd Roddle

Owd Roddle is based on an actual person whom Waugh had met at Smallbridge, near Rochdale. " 'Owd Roddle' is a broken-down village fuddler—perpetually racking his brains about 'another gill'. His appearance is more that of an Indian Fakeer than an English country gentleman.—A native of Smallbridge was asked, lately, what 'Roddle' did for his living, and he replied, 'Whaw, he wheels coals, and trails abeawt wi' his clogs loce [loose], an' may's a foo' [fool] of his-sel' for ale.' " (*Lancashire Sketches*, third edition, 1869, p. 129). The poem first appeared in the collected edition of Waugh's work.

Verse 2. Barmy slops: left-overs when the landlord brewed his own ale. Barm is yeast.

Owd Enoch

On the face of it this poem may seem heavily sentimental, but it is redeemed by its touches of humour, its lively imagery, and indeed by the delicate suggestion of the affection between two very old people. The moral of the closing verses is a familiar one in better known poetry but has seldom been expressed more effectively. The poem first appeared in the 1870 edition of Waugh's verse.

Ill life—ill luck

This poem represents a theme common in dialect poetry and elsewhere—the ridiculousness, and indeed the wrongness, of an old man marrying a young woman. No doubt its prevalence is connected with the ideal of cosy firesides and bonny children. In this case I am not sure that the point has been made. Perhaps "owd Bill at Kay's" should have been punished for his gay bachelor life by suffering a lonely or miserable old age, but "buxom Mall o' Pinders" does not sound to be altogether punishment.

This poem first appeared in the collected edition of Waugh's work.

Good neet

A kind of one-sided dialogue with strong moral overtones is again a common form in dialect poetry, especially when old people are imagined to be looking at their lives. Often the result is sickly-sentimental, but James Dawson's poem, which appeared in Harland's *Lancashire Lyrics*, has a certain dignity which is very appealing.

Thee an' me

Again a familiar moral is presented effectively, and with grim humour, by Laycock—especially perhaps in the final assertion that, despite everything, "thee and me" are friends.

Verse 8. Albert, hoop an' pin: an albert was a gentleman's watch chain, the hoop being the part to which the watch was fastened; the pin attached the chain to the waistcoat. There were double and single alberts.

Verse 9. Campin'; in Lancashire dialect "camping" means something more than the modern standard English sense. It really means going to somebody else's house and making yourself comfortable there. Hence heaven is our real home, but we "camp" for a time on earth (*cf*. "Friends are few when folks are poor," v. 1).

The poem shows signs of considerable revision, particularly the closing verse. In the earlier versions the penultimate verse ("Pack up thi albert") is missing altogether, and the last does not contain the very effective "campin' " image. This may indicate the particular, and somewhat uncharacteristic, care which Laycock seems to have taken with this poem—arguably one of the best he ever wrote.

Owd Fogey

This poem, reminiscent of "Bowton's Yard" in style, and to some extent in subject matter, is another reminder of Laycock's objection to strong drink and the close connection which grew up in the '60s and '70s between some dialect poets and the temperance movement. The version given here is from the 1875 edition of his poems.

Tha's noan so fur to tramp, owd friend

This short poem is taken from Laycock's essay "Lancashire Kesmus [Christmas] singin' fifty years sin'." Interestingly, it is in the same metre as "Bonny brid."

My piece is o bu' woven eawt

A famous dialect poem, and deservedly so. The comparison is skilfully drawn between the making of a life by a man or woman and the making of a piece of cloth by an old hand-loom weaver who at the end of the week had to take it to his employer for approval. The moral is obvious, but it is effectively and economically drawn.

Tim Bobbin's grave

One of the very few poems Samuel Bamford wrote in his native dialect. It appeared in *Hours in the Bowers* in 1834. I have placed it so far out of chronological order in this section of the anthology because it seems nicely to round things off, both thematically and historically.

"Tim Bobbin" (John Collier) was a celebrated dialect writer of the eighteenth century, the first man to establish dialect writing and make it respectable (*cf.* Introduction, p. 2). He was therefore regarded as a father figure by his successors, and there was already a traditional poem about "Tim Bobbin's grave" in existence when Bamford wrote this one. Similar poems were to follow later, including one by Ben Brierley on "Sam Bamford's grave," and a poem by the modern dialect writer Harvey Kershaw, "Lines to Tim Bobbin."

As might be guessed, Tim Bobbin had a reputation as a good companion and an enthusiastic drinker. His grave is still to be seen in Rochdale parish churchyard.

Notes on the writers

Samuel Bamford, 1788–1872. This famous radical was present at the Peterloo massacre and was imprisoned for a year afterwards. As a young man he had several jobs, at one time being a weaver, at another a sailor. Then he worked as a reporter, and for seven years was a doorkeeper at Somerset House in London. At the age of seventy he settled at Moston, near Manchester. Although he was keenly interested in dialect, and wrote a book entitled *The Dialect of South Lancashire*, most of his poetry is in standard English.

William Baron, 1865–1927. Baron was born at Blackpool but his family moved to Blackburn when he was five. At twelve he started work in the factory. In 1895 he moved to Stockport, and then in 1899 to Rochdale. From here, between 1909 and 1911, he edited his *Bill o' Jack's* monthly of dialect writing, most of which seems to have been his own work. He was a founder member of the Lancashire Author's Association in 1910.

Richard Rome Bealey, 1828–87. Bealey was born in Rochdale, and when his father died the family moved to Manchester. After an apprenticeship as a draper he started his own business. He was one of the founder members, along with Waugh and Brierley, of the Manchester Literary Club, but in 1878 he moved to Nottingham. Although during his lifetime he had a considerable reputation as a dialect poet, "My piece" seems far better than anything else he ever wrote.

William Billington, 1827–84. Billington is one of the most interesting of a group of writers centred around Blackburn, in north-east Lancashire. He was the son of a road contractor and worked in the mill from the age of eight. His family moved to Blackburn in 1839, and William got a job first as a doffer and then as a dandy-loom weaver.

During the Cotton Famine of the early 1860s he hawked his own books from door to door to make ends meet. Later he became a publican. He had a very unhappy second marriage, his wife leaving him after the birth of their son, and apparently, he became a heavy drinker.

Ben Brierley, 1825–96. Brierley was born in Failsworth. In early life he was a hand-loom weaver of velvet, but later became a journalist. In 1862 he went to London for a short time, but soon came back to Lancashire. He became well known as an author and reader of his own works, and established his own long-running *Ben Brierley's Journal*. He became a Manchester councillor and made a literary tour of America. In fact, along with Waugh, he was easily the most successful of the Lancashire dialect writers, and a statue to him was erected in Queen's Park, Manchester, after his death.

Joseph Burgess, 1853–1934. Burgess, like Brierley, was born in Failsworth, but he moved about a good deal in his youth in search of work. He was a part-timer in the mills at eight, and a full-timer at thirteen. His family finally settled in Middleton, and shortly after this he began to contribute poems to the *Oldham Chronicle*. It is interesting to note how much of his dialect poetry must have been written while he was still a teenager! In 1881 he left the mill, and Lancashire, to work as a journalist in the pioneer days of the labour movement. Further details of his life and examples of his verse can be found in his autobiography, *A Potential Poet?* (Ilford, 1927).

John Trafford Clegg, 1857–95. Clegg seems to me to be one of the best of the dialect poets in the generation immediately following Waugh and Laycock. He was born in Milnrow, but soon moved to Rochdale, and went to the grammar school there. He worked at a printing press with his brother, and then for a time in a cotton mill at Glossop which his father had bought. He was also a talented musician. He died in Bournemouth from TB at the age of thirty-seven. In 1890, interestingly enough, J. H. Wylie, a school inspector, suggested during a prize-giving speech in Rochdale that the Lancashire dialect should be taught as a subject in local elementary schools. He felt that a school version of Tim Bobbin's "Tummus and Meary" should be produced. Clegg joined in the ensuing correspondence in the *Rochdale Observer* with two letters written in dialect under his pen name, "Th Owd Weaver." He was very much against Wylie's idea, and his witty letters did a lot to stop it coming to anything. (*Cf.* Introduction, p. 2.)

James Dawson, Jnr, 1840–1906. James Dawson was the son of a farmer at Hartshead. As a young man he moved to Manchester and tried to make a career in literature. He became a friend of Waugh and a member of the Manchester Literary Club. He then went to work on the staff of a London newspaper, but on the death of his father returned to Hartshead. Most of his work, including *Facts and Fancies from the Farm* (1868), is in standard English.

Sam Fitton, 1868–1923. Fitton was born in Congleton, Cheshire, but when he was only two his parents moved to Rochdale. He worked in the mill, first as a doffer and then as a piecer, but he soon gained a reputation as a cartoonist and a public entertainer. It was for his own recitation that many of his poems were composed. Fitton seems to represent some later developments in Lancashire poetry, where it becomes quaint and humorous and begins to lose its directness. His wit and keenness of observation nevertheless raise his verse above the level of most of his contemporaries.

Samuel Laycock, 1826–93. Laycock was actually born in Yorkshire—in the Pennine village of Marsden. His father was a hand-loom weaver, and the only formal education Sam received, apart from going to Sunday school, was for a very short time when he was six years old. At the age of nine he went to work in a woollen mill in Marsden, and when he was eleven the family moved to Stalybridge. There Laycock started work in the cotton mills and eventually became a cloth looker. During the Cotton Famine of the early 1860s, however, he was thrown out of work. It was then that he wrote his most famous poems—the twelve "Lyrics of the Cotton Famine." Their success made him some money, and in 1868, being in poor health, he moved to Blackpool. He became curator of the Whitworth Institute in Fleetwood and enjoyed a reputation as a photographer.

Joseph Lees, 1748–1824. It seems likely that Lees was the author of "Jone o' Grinfilt" (*cf.* p. 127 above). He lived at Beckett Fold, Glodwick, where he was better known as Joseph o' Randall. He was a hand-loom weaver and schoolteacher. Apparently it was his custom to "study on his seatboard, and when he had thrown a few ideas into rhyme he stopt 'picking-o'er' and wrote it down" (*cf.* review of *Folk Song and Folk Speech of Lancashire* in the Harland manuscripts).

J. W. Mellor. A rather mysterious figure. Although under his pseudonym "Uncle Owdem" he published a great deal during the heyday of dialect writing in the 1860s, I have been unable to discover anything of his history.

E. Moss. This "E. Moss" is presumably Elijah Moss, who also wrote during the Cotton Panic a poem in standard English, "Our factory school," about a school at Higher Hurst. It was quoted in the contemporary "Reports of Factories" for the half-year ending 31 October 1862: *Parliamentary Papers, XVIII*, 1863, pp. 479–80 (*cf.* C. R. Fay, *Round about Industrial Britain*, 1830–60, Toronto, 1952, p. 109).

Joseph Ramsbottom, 1831–1901. Very little seems to be recorded about Joseph Ramsbottom, whose book *Phases of Distress: Lancashire Rhymes* was published towards the end of the American civil war in 1864. The editor of *Phases of Distress*, John Whittaker, "A Lancashire Lad," says that as boys both he and Ramsbottom were "toiling in the same dye-house" and that now both of them have "escaped from our former uncongenial life." His obituary in the *Manchester Guardian* (February 1901) records that he was a self-made man who "had overcome great difficulties in his early life." At one time he was a partner in a grey-cloth firm and was afterwards in a business of his own. In his earlier years he was a "familiar figure in the Manchester literary club" and when he died was said to have almost completed a "history of the labouring classes." There is no evidence that this was ever published. In his later years he was also a commercial contributor to the *Manchester Evening News*. "He was a man of native ability and kindly nature," says the *Guardian*. Apart from *Phases of Distress* very little of Ramsbottom's poetry seems to have survived. One or two of his poems were published in *Country Words*, a short-lived journal of 1866–67 (to which he also contributed a significant article in defence of dialect poetry), and one or two have appeared in various anthologies. But on the whole his work has been neglected, and as far as I know his poems of the Cotton Panic have never been anthologised, except for some incomplete extracts in Harland's contemporary *Lancashire Lyrics*.

John Scholes, 1808?–63. Although Scholes appears to have had a considerable local reputation, and his poetry in dialect was singled out by *The Atheneum* in its review of Harland's *Lancashire Lyrics* (February 1866), it is hard to discover much about his life. After failing as a hat manufacturer he appears to have earned a living by writing for the local press in Rochdale. He died of TB at Smallbridge, near Rochdale.

James Standing, 1848–78. Standing was born in Cliviger, near Burnley, and was working for a bobbin-maker before he was eight. In his short life he had an incredible number of different jobs—including school teacher and auctioneer. Nevertheless he still found time to teach himself French and German. From 1873 to 1877 he published the *Lancashire and Yorkshire Comic, Historic and Poetic Almanack*, which had a wide circulation in the Burnley area. He died aged thirty, shortly after the death of both his wife and his child. An interesting article on him, "Folk speech of the

Lancashire and Yorkshire border", can be found in Stansfield's *Essays and Sketches* (1897).

Mary Thomason, 1863–1937. Mary Thomason was for many years a teacher at a Wesleyan primary school in Leigh. Her book of poetry *Warp and Weft* was not published until after her death.

Edwin Waugh, 1817–90. The most famous and successful of the dialect poets was the son of a shoemaker and was born in Rochdale. His father died when he was nine, and for a time he and his mother were so poor that they had to live in a cellar. He had no formal education, but from the age of twelve he worked for Thomas Holden, a Rochdale bookseller, and this gave him the chance to educate himself. While still a young man he worked as a journeyman printer and travelled all over England but eventually came back to his old job in Rochdale. In 1847 he was appointed assistant secretary to the Lancashire Public Schools Association and went to work in Manchester. A diary he kept at this time, now in the Manchester Central Library, shows that his married life was rather unhappy, and he became separated from his wife. This may help to explain why so much of his poetry is concerned with the blessings of a happy home! In 1855, when he was working as a traveller for a Manchester printing firm, he published his first book, *Sketches of Lancashire Life and Localities*. A year later his first dialect poem appeared; this was the one that made him famous, "Come whoam to thi childer an' me." By 1860 he was doing well enough to become a full-time writer, and in 1881, when he was already a sick man, he was given a Civil List pension of £90 a year. He died at New Brighton and was buried at Kersal, where he had lived for most of his later years.

Harry Buckley Whitehead, 1890–1966. Whitehead was born at Diggle, near Oldham. He started work in the mill at thirteen and remained a mill worker until his retirement in the early 1950s. In 1963 his *Rhymes of a Village Poet* was published, but the book is not readily available.

The Wilsons

Michael Wilson and two of his seven sons, Thomas and Alexander, gained quite a reputation as poets in the Manchester area in the first half of the nineteenth century. There were four printed editions of their works between 1842 and 1866, but, even so, many of their songs were never written down or have been lost.

Michael Wilson, 1763–1840. The son of a hand-loom weaver who had moved to Manchester from Edinburgh. He himself worked as a printer and as a furniture broker. He had a reputation for being left-wing, a "Jacobin" in politics.

Thomas Wilson, ?–1852. The second son, Thomas, went as a boy to Chetham's Hospital School in Manchester. He was a dealer in smallware, and during the Napoleonic wars he was put in prison for six months for smuggling gold. Harland (*The Songs of the Wilsons*, 1865) suggests that this was unfair treatment, since many Manchester businessmen were engaged in smuggling at the time without being punished. His date of birth seems uncertain, but was presumably some time in the 1780s.

Alexander Wilson, 1804–46. The youngest of the seven sons. He became the publicist of the family by producing printed editions of their poems during the 1840s. He was also a self-taught animal painter of considerable local fame, his best known painting being "The Manchester rushcart." He died suddenly, and was buried at Cheetham Hill cemetery, where the well known local poet Elijah Ridings inscribed an epitaph for him (*cf.* E. Ridings, *The Lancashire Muse*).

Ammon Wrigley, 1862–1946. This Saddleworth poet gained a great local reputation during his lifetime as an antiquarian and a writer. More or less self-educated, a half-timer in the mill at the age of nine, he became famous enough for a literary club, "The Ammon Wrigley Fellowship," to form round him during his lifetime, and to have had a radio broadcast about him on his death. He was a close friend of Sam Fitton, but he actually wrote very little of his poetry in dialect form, preferring to use standard English to sing the delights of the moors near Saddleworth.

Bibliography

Works

Bamford, S., *Homely Rhymes, Poems and Reminiscences*, Manchester, 1864.
Baron, W., *Bits o'Broad Lancashire*, Blackburn, 1888.
—*Echoes from the Loom*, Rochdale, 1903.
Bealey, R. R., *After-business Jottings*, London, undated
Billington, W., *Lancashire Songs*, Blackburn, 1883.
Brierley, B., *Spring Blossoms and Autumn Leaves*, Manchester, 1893.
Burgess, J., *A Potential Poet?* Ilford, 1927.
Collier, J., *The Miscellaneous Works of Tim Bobbin*, Manchester, 1775.
Clegg, J. T., *Reaund bi' t' Derby*, Rochdale, 1890.
—The Works of John Trafford Clegg, (two vols.), Rochdale, 1895, 1898.
Fitton, S., *Gradely Lancashire*, Stalybridge, 1929.
Laycock, S., *Lancashire Rhymes*, Manchester, 1864.
—*Lancashire Songs*, Manchester, 1866.
—*Poems and Songs*, Manchester, 1875.
—*Warblings fro' an Owd Songster*, Oldham, 1893, 1903.
—*The Collected Writings*, Oldham, 1900, 1907.
Mellor, J. W., *Poems in the Lancashire Dialect*, Manchester, 1865.
Ramsbottom, J., *Phases of Distress*, Manchester, 1864.
Standing, J., *Echoes from a Lancashire Vale*, Manchester, 1873.
Thomason, M., *Warp and Weft: Cuts from a Lancashire Loom*, Leigh, 1938.
Waugh, E., *Poems and Lancashire Songs*, first edition, Manchester, 1859; second
    edition, Manchester, 1861; third edition, Manchester 1870.
—*Lancashire Songs*. Manchester, 1865.
—*Collected Works*, vols. 10–11, Manchester, 1881–89; 1892–93.
Wrigley, A., *Songs of a Moorland Parish*, Saddleworth, 1912.

Anthologies

Andrews, W., *North Country Poets* (two vols.), London, 1889.
Bennett, J., *A Lancashire Miscellany of Dialect Verse*, Oldham, 1960.
Case, R. H., *Lancashire in Prose and Verse*, London, 1930.
Gaskel, *Gaskel's Original Comic Songs*, Manchester, undated
Graham, J., *Dialect Songs of the North*, London, 1910.
Halliwell, J. O., *Tha Palatine Anthology*, London, 1850.
Harland, J., *Ballads and Songs of Lancashire*, London, 1865; second edition (revised), 1875; third edition (revised), 1882.
—*The Songs of the Wilsons*, London, 1865; second edition, 1866.
—*Lancashire Lyrics*, London, 1866.
Hill, S., *Old Lancashire Songs and their Singers*, Stalybridge, 1898.
Hull, G., *Poets and Poetry of Blackburn*, Blackburn, 1902.
—*English Lyrics and Lancashire Songs*, Preston, 1922.
Pickles, W., *My North Countrie*, London, 1955.
Procter, R. W., *Gems of Thought and Flowers of Fancy*, London, 1855.
Ridings, E., *The Lancashire Muse*, Manchester, 1853.
Rogerson, J. B., *The Festive Wreath*, Manchester, 1842.
Whittaker, G. H., *A Lancashire Garland*, Stalybridge, 1936.
—*Some Stalybridge Songs and their Singers*, Stalybridge, 1944.
Wilson, A., *Songs of the Wilsons*, Manchester, 1842; second edition, 1847.
Yates, M., *A Lancashire Anthology*, London, 1923.

Records

A Lancashire Mon, Topic 12 TS 236, 1973.
Deep Lancashire, Topic 12 T1 88, 1968.
Oldham's Burning Sands, Topic 12 TS 206, 1971.
Owdham Edge, Topic 12 T 204, 1970.
Steam Whistle Ballads, Topic 12 T 104,
Trans-Pennine, Topic 12 TS 215, 1971.

Literary criticism and history

Athenaum, No. 1966 (1 July 1865), review of Harland's *Ballads and Songs of Lancashire*.
—No. 1998 (10 February 1866), review of *Lancashire Lyrics* and *The Songs of the Wilsons*.
Axon, W. E. A., *Folk Song and Folk Speech of Lancashire*, Manchester, 1870. "A Lancashire poet—Samuel Laycock," *Manchester Literary Club Papers*, 1891, pp. 355–66.
Anon., "Edwin Waugh," *Manchester Literary Club Papers*, 1890, pp. 197–204.
—Memorial notice for Laycock, *Manchester Literary Club Papers*, 1894, pp. 459–61.

Croston, J., *The Late John Harland*, London, 1868.
Derby, T., "Folk songs of Lancashire," *Manchester Literary Club Papers*, 1913, pp. 79–99.
Evans, J., *Lancashire Authors and Orators*, London, 1850.
Harland, J., "Songs of the working classes," No. 1, *Manchester Guardian*, 4 December 1839.
—"Songs of the working classes," No. 2. *Manchester Guardian*, 24 December 1839.
Higson, C. E., *Jone o' Grinfilt and Oldham Rushbearing*, Oldham, 1926.
Lazarus, S. H., "Life and times of Ben Brierley, 1825–96," unpublished thesis: Manchester Library, Manchester, 1964.
Lloyd, A. L., *Folk Song in England*, London, 1967.
Milner, G., *The Dialect of Lancashire considered as a Vehicle for Poetry*, Manchester, 1874.
—"Edwin Waugh," *Manchester Literary Club Papers*, 1893.
Mortimer, J., "Some Lancashire rhymes," *Manchester Literary Club Papers*, 1890, pp. 55–65.
Muschamp, R., "Richard Rome Bealey," *Transactions of the Rochdale Literary and Scientific Society*, 1919–22, vol. XIV, pp. 6–10.
Procter, R. W., *Literary Reminiscences and Gleanings*, London, 1860.
Ramsbottom, J., "Writing in the dialect," *Country Words*, 15 December 1866, pp. 104–5.
Stansfield, A., *Essays and Sketches*, 1897.
Swann, J. R., *Lancashire Authors*, Accrington, 1924.
Vicinus, M., "The study of nineteenth-century working-class poetry," in *The Politics of Literature*, ed. L. Kampf and P. Lauter, New York, pp. 322–55.
—"The literary voices of an industrial town, 1810–70," in *The Victorian City*, ed. H. J. Dyos and M. Wolff, London, 1973, vol II, pp. 739–61.
—*The Industrial Muse*, London, 1974.

Background books

Dialect

Bamford, S., *The Dialect of South Lancashire*, Manchester, 1854.
Brook, G. L., *English Dialects*, London, 1963.
Gaskell, W., *Two Lectures on the Lancashire Dialect*, London, 1854.
Halliwell, J. O., *Dictionary of Archaic and Provincial Words* (two vols.), London, 1847.
Nodal, J. H., and Milner, G., *A Glossary of the Lancashire Dialect*, Manchester, 1875.

History

Axon, W. E. A., *Lancashire Gleanings*, Manchester, 1883.
Axon, E., *Bygone Lancashire*, London, 1892.
Bamford, S., *Walks in South Lancashire*, Manchester, 1844.
Bateson, H., *History of Oldham*, Oldham, 1949.

Bythell, D., *The Handloom Weavers*, Cambridge, 1969.
Fay, C. R., *Round About Industrial Britain, 1830–60*, Toronto, 1952.
Foster, J., *Class Struggle and the Industrial Revolution*, London, 1974.
Gaskell, E., *Mary Barton*, London, 1848.
Hayes, L. M., *Reminiscences of Manchester*, London, 1905.
Henderson, W. O., *The Lancashire Cotton Famine*, Manchester, 1934.
Henslow, A. F., *Cotton and the want of it*, London, 1863.
Hill, S., *Bygone Stalybridge*, Stalybridge, 1907.
Mattley, R. D., *Annals of Rochdale*, Rochdale, 1899.
Newbigging, T., *Lancashire Characters and Places*, Manchester, 1891.
Procter, R. W., *Memorials of Bygone Manchester*, Manchester, 1880.
Swindells, T., *Manchester Streets and Manchester Men*, Manchester, 1908.
Tomlinson, W., *Bye-ways of Manchester Life*, Manchester, 1887.
Waugh, E., *Collected Works*, Manchester, 1881–9.

Bibliographies

Axon, W. E. A., *The Literature of the Lancashire Dialect*, London, 1870.
English Dialect Dictionary, List of Lancashire and Cheshire books, Manchester, 1895.
English Dialect Library, *Catalogue*, Manchester, 1880.
Humphreys, A. L., *A Handbook to County Bibliography*, London, 1917.
Skeat, W. W., and Nodal, J. H., *Bibliographical List: English Dialect Society*, London, 1877.
Sutton, C. W., *A List of Lancashire Authors*, Manchester, 1876.

Journals and magazines

Baron, W., *Bill o' Jacks Lancashire Monthly*, Rochdale, 1909–11.
Brierley, B., *Ben Brierley's Journal*, Manchester, 1869–91.
City News Notes and Queries, Manchester, 1878–90.
Country Words, Manchester, 1866–67.
Manchester Literary Club, *Proceedings*, 1873–74.
Papers, 1875 onwards.
The Palatine Notebook, Manchester, 1881–84.

Library collections

Blackburn Library:
Baron, J. T., Album of 745 rhymes.
Chetham's Library, Manchester:
Axon, W. E. A., Collection of broadsides and ballads.
Harris Library, Preston:
Collection of broadsides.
Manchester Library:
Broadsheet collection (catalogued 427.72 L43).
Green, J. A., Axonana.
Harland, J., Harland manuscripts.
—Harland scrapbooks.

Lancashire dialect pieces (catalogued 427.72 L47).
Manchester scrapbook (catalogued 942.7389 M122).
Waugh, E., Diary, 1847–51.
—Commonplace book.
Rochdale Library:
Brierley, H. (Dr), Original record book.

Index

Poets

First lines

Notes on the poems will be found at the pages shown in brackets

A merry little doffer lad, 18 (130)
An owd maid aw shall be, for aw'm eighteen to-morn, 47 (135)
As I coom trailin' whoam fro' th' town, 118 (148)
At number one, i' Bowton's Yard, 20 (131)
Aw dunnot reckon aw con preytch, 75 (141)
Aw've just bin a havin' a peep at th' farm-heawse, 21 (131)
Aw've just mended th' fire wi' a cob, 64 (138)
Aw've turned mi bit o' garden o'er, 107 (147)

Come, Betty, lass, it's Rachda' Wakes, 37 (134)
Come, Billy, come; dost yer yon bell?, 86 (142)
Come carders an' spinners an' wayvers as weel, 86 (142)
Come Dick, an' Nan, an' Davy, 31 (132)
Come, lasses, let's cheer up, an' sing, 109 (147)
Come, lively lads an' laughin maids, 38 (134)
Come, Mary, link thi arm i' mine, 50 (136)
Come, Mary, put mi pit clogs by, 94 (144)

Deawn i' th' shed on a summer's day, 90 (144)

Eawr Joe he's started coortin' neaw, 59 (138)
Eh, dear, I'm welly off my chump!, 78 (141)
Eh, dear; there's bin some change in, 57 (138)
Eh, dear! what weary toimes are these, 100 (146)
Eh, Nan, Lord bless an' save us o, 36 (133)
Eh! Sam, whatever doesto meean?, 67 (139)
Er Johnny gi's his mind to books, 15 (129)

For fooak at's slaves to t' factory bell, 91 (144)
Fro heawrs to days—a dhreary length—, 105 (147)

Good law, how things are alter'd now, 12 (128)
Good Lorjus days, what times are these, 87 (142)
Good neet, owd friend! aw wish thee well, 120 (149)

Heaw slow these weary weeks dhrag on, 110 (147)
Heigh! Hall o' Nabs, an' Sam, an' Sue, 33 (133)
Heigh, Mary; run for the fryin'-pon, 68 (140)
Hi thi, Jenny, lyev thi loom, 51 (137)

I stood beside Tim Bobbin's grave, 125 (150)
I'm a poor cotton weaver as many one knows, 11 (128)
I't shed, wheer aw'm toilin' an' slavin', 56 (137)
It's Dreighlsdin wakes, un' wey're comin' to teawn, 30 (132)
It's hard to ceawer i' th' chimney nook, 104 (146)
It's run an' jump an' hop an' skip, 43 (134)

Jack, goo peawn thi fiddle, 35 (133)

Meight when we're hungry, 64 (138)
My "piece" is o' bu' woven eawt, 124 (150)

Now, aw me gud gentles, an yau won tarry, 29 (132)

Owd Enoch o' Dans laid his pipe deawn o' th' hob, 117 (148)
Owd Fogey lives i' Turner's Fowd, 122 (149)
Owd Roddle wur tattert an' torn, 116 (148)

Sam, at Jack o' Neddurs, wur tir't o' livin' single life, 46 (135)
Says Jone to his woife on a whot summer's day, 10 (127)
Shoddy, shoddy, shoddy, that's the sooart to spin, 89 (143)

Tha'rt livin' at this country seat, 120 (149)
Tha'rt welcome, little bonny brid, 73 (140)
Tha's noan so fur to tramp owd friend, 124 (149)
The dule's i' this bonnet o' mine, 48 (135)
Th' wynt blows keen through th' shiverin' thorns, 65 (139)
Ther never wur such times as these, 108 (147)
There's nobuddy knows wod we'n gooan through, 112 (147)
Ther's tay kettle singin' a tune, 72 (140)
To yo' who read as well as run, 40 (134)
Tum Rindle lope fro' the chimbley nook, 16 (130)
'Twur on a bitter winter neet, 70 (140)

We han some funny folk i' Cotton Fowd, 23 (131)
We're werkin lads frae Lankisheer, 98 (145)
Well, want yo pins or neelds today, 102 (146)
When I had wark, and brass to spend, 14 (129)
When I'd finished off my work, 83 (142)
When mi faythur fust wur wed, 54 (137)
When t' factory loces uv a neet, 93 (144)

Yo gentlemen o with yor heawnds an' yor parks, 19 (130)
Yo'n throuble wi' childer fro' th' cayther to th' grave, 53 (137)
Yoh munnut come agen hard times, 95 (144)